Communicate 1

English for social interaction

Keith Morrow and Keith Johnson
Centre for Applied Language Studies, University of Reading

with drawings by Martin Salisbury

Cambridge University Press
Cambridge
London   New York   New Rochelle
Melbourne   Sydney

Published by the Press Syndicate of the University of Cambridge
The Pitt Building, Trumpington Street, Cambridge CB2 1RP
32 East 57th Street, New York, NY 10022, U.S.A.
296 Beaconsfield Parade, Middle Park, Melbourne 3206, Australia

© Cambridge University Press 1979

First published 1979

Printed in Great Britain at the
Alden Press, Oxford

ISBN 0 521 21850 0 Student's Book 1
ISBN 0 521 21849 7 Teacher's Book 1
ISBN 0 521 21848 9 Cassette 1

ISBN 0 521 22140 4 Student's Book 2
ISBN 0 521 22740 1 Teacher's Book 2
ISBN 0 521 22747 X Cassette 2

Acknowledgements

The authors and publishers are grateful to the following for permission to reproduce
illustrations:
Jon Harris (pages 16, 97, 100, 120, 123);
London Transport (page 111).

Cover photograph by Richard Greenhill

Design and art direction by Peter Ducker

Contents

To the student

Who is *Communicate* for?

It's for adult learners of English. It's for people who have already studied English for a short time (maybe at school or at university). It's for people who want to learn to use English in Britain.

What does *Communicate* do?

It shows you how to do things in English: for example, it shows you how to find out things, how to ask people to do things, how to suggest things to people. It also shows you what to say in situations: when you meet a person for the first time, when you say good-bye, when someone invites you to dinner. And it tells you a lot about living in Britain: how to use the telephones, how to book a taxi, how to get help if your car breaks down.

How does *Communicate* work?

Communicate is not really a grammar book, so don't be surprised if the exercises seem strange at first. Often you will work in pairs or in groups. Again this will perhaps seem strange. But we want you to listen and to speak in English as much as possible. We want you to learn to use the language to communicate.

　　We hope you enjoy it.

Keith Morrow
Keith Johnson

Unit 1 Introductory

A Doing things in English

1 Mr and Mrs Jones, Janet, Sue, John and Simon are all doing the same thing. What is it? Who do you think they are speaking or writing to? How well do they know that person?

WE'RE HAVING A PARTY NEXT THURSDAY. WOULD YOU LIKE TO COME?

MR and MRS JONES

Mr and Mrs F. A. Jones request the pleasure of Mr Michael Ashby's company at

JOHN AND I ARE GOING TO LONDON ON TUESDAY, AND WE THOUGHT YOU MIGHT LIKE TO JOIN US. YOU'D BE VERY WELCOME...

BY THE WAY, SANDRA. ARE YOU FREE NEXT THURSDAY? THERE'S A DANCE ON AT THE TOWN HALL. I THOUGHT WE COULD GO TOGETHER.

HEY, JOHN. HOW ABOUT A QUICK DRINK BEFORE LUNCH?

JOHN

SIMON

2   What do you think Jane, Arthur, Mike, Alison and Mr Hall are doing?

JANE

ARTHUR

MIKE

ALISON

MR HALL

Where are the speakers? Who are they talking to? How well do they know the
person they're talking to? Think about what is happening.

3   Sometimes it's quite difficult to know what people are really saying. Here are some more sentences. They all look like questions.

Is that right?
Why don't you sit down?
Is this your hat?
Have you met Roger?
Could you close the door?
Have you finished with the salt?
Is that really the time?
Isn't that beautiful?

But are they really questions? Here are some things the speakers could be saying. Which sentences mean the same as the ones above?

I'm going to introduce you to Roger.
I must go now.
I want you to sit down.
Please pass the salt.
It really is beautiful.
Please close the door.
I think you've forgotten your hat.
I'm sure that's wrong.

4   i)   What would *you* say in these situations?
   a)   You're in the street and you want to know what the time is. You've left your watch at home. You go up to a stranger and say. . .
   b)   You're in a shop and you accidentally hit someone with your bag. You turn to the person and say. . .
   c)   Someone you met recently invites you to dinner at his house next week. You want to go, so you say. . .
   d)   You want to catch the train to London. You're at the station, but you're not sure which platform the train goes from. You go up to a porter and say. . .
   e)   Your best friend has just said something very stupid. You want to tell him that you disagree strongly. So you say. . .

   ii)   You've just practised doing these things – in which sentences?
      accepting an invitation
      disagreeing
      asking for information
      saying sorry

   iii)   Think of some other ways of doing these things. When would you use them? In what situations?

▶   Did you find this exercise difficult? You have already learned quite a lot of English grammar, and you know lots of English words. But grammar and vocabulary aren't everything. You must also learn to *do things in English* – like accepting invitations, disagreeing, asking for information, saying sorry.

In this book you will learn how to do these and other things with your English.

B   Doing the right thing

1   How much do you know about the way the British live and behave? Do this quiz.

You're in Britain

1   You're visiting the house of a British friend. It's very beautiful. Do you:
   a) tell him how beautiful it is?
   b) ask how much it cost?
   c) ask if he'll take you round every room?

2   You've arranged to meet a friend at 2.00. But you miss the train and you know you'll be at least two hours late. Do you:
   a) decide not to meet your friend, and phone him the next day?
   b) phone him, apologise and tell him you'll be late?
   c) decide not to phone, and just arrive late?

3   A British acquaintance is having dinner at your house. His plate is empty. You offer him more food and he says no. Do you:
   a) keep offering until he says yes?
   b) just put the food on his plate without asking again?
   c) offer once more, then give up if he still says no?

4   You meet a British friend in the street. You last saw him two days ago. Do you:
   a) just say hello?
   b) say hello and shake his hand?
   c) put your arm round his shoulder and slap him on the back?

5   You're at a party and have just been introduced to someone. While you are talking he mentions that his wife is not at the party. Do you:
   a) ask where his wife is?
   b) change the subject?
   c) ask if he gets on well with his wife?

6   You're having dinner at a British friend's house. You don't like the food he gives you at all. When he offers you some more, do you say:
   a) 'No thanks. I don't like it'?
   b) 'It was lovely but I really can't. . .'?
   c) 'No, I don't want any more'?

7   You're in a railway carriage. There's someone else you don't know in the carriage. It's very hot and you'd like the window open. Do you:
   a) open it without asking the other person?
   b) ask the other person to open the window?
   c) ask the other person if you can open the window?

How did you score?

1	a)5	b)0	c)2		5	a)2	b)5	c)0
2	a)0	b)5	c)0		6	a)0	b)5	c)1
3	a)1	b)0	c)5		7	a)0	b)2	c)5
4	a)5	b)2	c)0					

Your knowledge of British life

35–30 marks Well done, a good score. But don't be too confident. The quiz was really quite easy.

29–20 marks Not bad, but there's still a lot to learn.

19–10 marks You've got a lot to learn about British life.

9–0 marks   Oh dear! You'd better study this book very hard.

2 In the quiz you saw seven situations. Now imagine you are in your own country, and everyone you are talking to is the same nationality as you. What would you say or do in these seven situations? Compare it with what the British would do.

3 Does anything about the way British people behave seem strange to you? Think about how they behave in shops, railway stations, restaurants and other places. Is it different from the way people in your country behave? What do you think British people would find strange about life in your country?

▶ Grammar and vocabulary certainly aren't everything! If you want to communicate with British people properly, you must know about their way of life (even if you do not agree with the way they live).
   In this book you will learn what British people say and do in different situations.

Unit 2 Introductory

A Doing things in English

1 JULIAN

TREVOR

GRAHAM

DR ADAMS

ANNE

MARTIN

What are these people doing?

Julian		giving an order
Graham		saying hello
Trevor	is	asking for something
Dr Adams		saying goodbye
Anne		offering to help
Martin		

In these pictures you can see there is more than one way of doing the same thing.
Which way is better for each picture? Why? When can the other way be used?

▶ When you do things in English – like giving an order, saying hello, asking for something, saying goodbye, offering help – you must make sure what you say is right for the person you are talking to.

2 i) Here are some more examples of saying the same thing in different ways. First of all look at these:

I want to see you.
Open the window.
Don't smoke here.
You're wrong.
What?
I don't believe you.
Be quiet.

Which of these sentences mean the same as the ones above?

Are you sure that's true?
Smoking is not allowed, I'm afraid.
Would you mind making less noise.
Could I see you for a moment?
I'm not sure I agree with you.
Would you open the window, please?
I'm afraid I didn't catch what you said.

What is the difference between these ways of saying the same thing? Which ones are more polite? When would you use each?

▶ We are usually *polite* when we speak to strangers, and more *direct* when we speak to friends.

ii) Are these expressions polite or direct?

What time is it?
Could I borrow a cigarette please?
I wonder if that's right.
Nonsense!
I want five 10p stamps.
I hope I'm not disturbing you.
I'm not sure I really agree with that.
I was wondering if you could lend me £5.

Do you use different ways to talk to friends and strangers in your own language? Think about the differences.

3 Listen to these sentences on tape.
Are the men: a) interested   b) surprised   c) doubtful   d) bored?

JAMES: I bought a new coat today.
DAVID: Really.   (a b c d)

PAULINE: I saw Mary and Fred in town.
MIKE: Really.   (a b c d)

RITA: I had coffee with my mother.
PAUL: Really.   (a b c d)

SALLY: Shall we go to the theatre tonight?
ALAN: Maybe.   (a b c d)

LIZ: Do you want to wash the car tomorrow?
TONY: Maybe   (a b c d)

JILL: My mother says she likes your new coat.
EDDY: Oh.   (a b c d)

CHRISTINE: Bill phoned this afternoon about the football match.
FRANK: Oh.   (a b c d)

▶   You can see that in English, the same words can express different feelings. It depends *how* we say them. You must learn *what* to say, and also *how* to say it.
Expressing your feelings, and understanding others who are expressing their feelings – these are also things you must learn to do in English.

B Saying the right thing

1 In unit 1 we looked at some of the things British people say and do in different situations. Do you know what to say in these situations?

a) You're in a restaurant and you want to have a steak. You like steaks which are not cooked too much. What would you ask for?

b) You need 2p to make a phone call. But you only have a pound note. Perhaps your friend can help. What would you ask him for?

c) You want to go by train to London. You'll be returning the same day (by train). You go to the station. What kind of a ticket do you ask for?

d) You have an account with a bank in Britain. You want to get details of the money you have paid in and taken out of your account recently. What do you ask the bank for?

e) You're in Bournemouth and you want to phone a friend in London. You want your friend to pay for the call. You go into a phone box and dial the operator. What kind of a call do you ask for?

2   What we say depends on *where* we are.

i)   Where do you think people might say these things:

a) A pint of bitter, please.	At a garage?
b) Two singles to Brighton, please.	At a station?
c) Number, please.	On the telephone?
d) Five of 4-star, please.	In a pub?
e) Where would you like the parting?	At the hairdresser's?

ii)   What about these? Where are the people who are speaking?

I'm afraid it's engaged.
Here is the new single from the Dreamers.
What's your nationality?
Time, gentleman, please.
Twenty King Size, please.
How would you like the money?
Could I have the bill, please?
The station, please.

3   What we say also depends on *what* we are talking about.

i)   What do you think these people are talking about?

a) Quite nice for the time of year.	a car?
b) It melts in your mouth.	a football match?
c) It's the latest sports model.	a book?
d) They scored again just after half time.	the weather?
e) It's out in paperback now.	some food?

ii)   What about these? What are the people talking about?

It's a bit overdone.
Yes, but the ending was a bit strange.
It does 0–100 in 12.6 secs.
It's got a stereo cassette deck as well.
It only cost £2 a metre
I prefer it black.
He won the first set 6–1.

iii) Here are parts of some advertisements taken from British newspapers. What do you think is being advertised? Can you fill in the missing words?

1 *Our new .... is designed ultra-slim to shave superbly close. It's as easy as shaving with your finger-tips.*

2 *A fine brushed chrome finish gives our .... a sophisticated look, and it's a pleasure to write with too. Inside a pump like a tiny heart forces ink to the point, so it writes at any angle, even upside down.*

3 *Every stage of life brings new responsibilities. You need the sound protection of an .... company to help you meet them as they come along. We can provide it through our range of specially designed policies.*

4 *Gently chilled, this fresh delicate .... brings the taste of good food into clear focus.*

5 *......... mixed with gin or vodka. One of the world's classical aperitifs. And after dinner you can stay with it all night. Some people have even been known to have it before and after lunch. Before and after sailing, golf, riding. Before and after just about anything.*

6 *Choose any three of the many .... featured here for a total of £1 plus 80p towards postage and packing. That's our special offer to you. Then every month we'll send you advance information about many more new books by famous authors. Fiction. Crafts. History. Travel. Gardening. Just about every subject under the sun. And most of them well under the publisher's prices.*

7 *Now the Underground brings Heathrow Airport to London's doorstep. The new Heathrow Central Station connects the Piccadilly Line to all three Heathrow Terminals. So you can get from the London Underground to your departure lounge, under cover all the way. The journey from Piccadilly Circus to the heart of Heathrow takes 40 minutes. With a frequent service, trains every 4 minutes in peak hours. Take the .... to Heathrow Airport. It's the only way to fly.*

8 *Give somebody one of our .... for Christmas and you might end up inside it.*

Unit 3

Arriving in Britain

A   Immigration control and customs

1   Practise these questions:

How would you reply?

Practise these replies:

Now practise the questions and replies together.

★   U.K. (United Kingdom) is the official name for the political unit which consists of England, Wales, Scotland and Northern Ireland.

2 i) In this conversation, Mary is introducing her cousin Adrian to her neighbour, Mrs Collins. Try to complete the sentences using words you have heard in the dialogues.

MARY: I'd .... introduce my cousin Adrian.

ADRIAN: How .... do, Mrs Collins.

MRS COLLINS: Hello, Adrian. I'm .... you.

ii) Practise introducing people:

Introduce	your classmate Ahmed your sister Carla your landlady, Mrs Horne your friend, Ron your teacher, Mr Day your girlfriend Sally your neighbour, Mrs Gorst your brother, Alberto	to	Mrs Adams Paul Mr Fletcher Mary Mrs Williams Simon Mrs Roberts Jane

3 i) Here are some questions people might ask when you're first introduced to them:

Where are you from?
Are you a student?
Are you here on holiday?
Are you going to be here long?

How would *you* answer these questions?

ii) Practise introducing people in your class. Ask them about themselves.

4 What do *you* say when you want to start a conversation with someone you don't know? Imagine you're at a party. Three students in your class will pretend to be these people:

A

You've never met
this person before.

His accent tells you he's not English. He sounds Spanish or French.

You could ask him where he lives. But 'where do you live?' sounds a little rude. Perhaps you could find out whether he lives nearby, or has a long journey home.

He may know someone at the party whom you also know. If you can find out then you can talk about the mutual friend.

Ask him questions to find out these things. Then decide who he is: Antonio Vargas, Carlos Alonzo or Jean Baptiste?

ANTONIO VARGAS comes from Spain. He lives quite near the place where the party is being held, but doesn't know anyone else at the party.

CARLOS ALONZO is Spanish. He lives quite near the place where the party's being held, and all his friends are there.

JEAN BAPTISTE comes from Paris. He doesn't know anyone else at the party and lives about fifteen miles away from the place where it's being held.

B

You think you've met this person before but you can't remember when.

At first you're sure he's a teacher at the college where you're studying – Prince Albert College.

Then you think he's a student at the university, where you have many friends.

Or maybe he lived in Manchester when you were there last year.

Ask questions, and decide who he is: Paul Richards, Alan Reid or John Denny?

PAUL RICHARDS teaches maths at Prince Albert College. He's lived in Winton (where the party's being held) all his life, but he never goes up to the university there.

ALAN REID has many friends at the University of Winton. He works as an engineer in a local factory, and has never been to Manchester.

JOHN DENNY is now an engineer working in a local factory. He used to study at Manchester University. He never goes to the university in Winton.

C

You've never met
this person before.

The party has been organised by the tennis club. Perhaps she's a member.

The tennis club has parties every year. This is the first time you've been, but perhaps she comes every year.

Or maybe she knows your friend Kate. Kate's at this party, and knows lots of people.

Ask questions and decide who she is: Sally Morton, Angela Dickinson or Jane Donaldson?

SALLY MORTON is a member of the tennis club. She always goes to tennis club parties, but doesn't know Kate.

ANGELA DICKINSON always goes to tennis club parties with her friend Kate. Angela is a member of the tennis club.

JANE DONALDSON knows Kate and has been to tennis club parties before. She doesn't play tennis herself, and isn't a member of the club.

Student A

Pretend to be this person. You're at a party and someone asks you questions. Tell them what they want to know.

You come from Spain (Madrid actually).

You don't know anyone else at the party. The friend who invited you has already gone home.

You live quite near the place where the party is being held, so you don't have a long journey home.

Student B

Pretend to be this person. You're at a party and someone asks you questions. Tell them what they want to know.

You are an engineer and you work in a local factory. You lived in Manchester last year, and you've never been to the university in the town where you are living.

Student C

Pretend to be this person. You're at a party and someone asks you questions. Tell them what they want to know.

You play tennis a lot, and you're a member of the tennis club. You always come to tennis club parties with your friend Kate.

5 English names can sometimes be confusing. And difficult to pronounce! Are these first names or surnames? Decide, then practise pronouncing them.

David   Steve
Thompson   Hughes
Stevens   Williams
Anne   Ian
Hugh   Jackie

Which of these do you use with Mr, Mrs, Miss, Ms?
When do you introduce someone by their first name?

Unit 5

People

A Polite talk

1 What kind of questions can you ask people when you meet them for the first time?

Practise these questions:

How would you reply?

Practise these replies:

Now practice the questions and replies together.

★ You can't actually start a conversation with these questions, but they show the sort of things that English people talk about with strangers. Never ask direct questions about money: e.g. 'How much do you earn?' 'How much did this cost?'

33

2 Antonio Varrona is an Italian who has applied for a scholarship to come and study engineering in Britain. Here are the details he gives in his application:

```
Antonio Varrona              Marital Status:   Single


Nationality:   Italian       Date of Birth: 30/11/50


Education

1961-9     Secondary School (liceo tecnico, Pisa)
1969-73    University of Pisa (B.Sc in Engineering)


Appointments

1973-4     Engineer employed by I.B.M., Pisa.
1974-present.  Engineer employed by D.O.W. Chemicals,
                 Livorno.
Other interests:  Football, fishing, cookery.
Other information
I would like to win this scholarship because I
wish to apply for the post of chief engineer
at D.O.W. Chemicals, Livorno.
```

i) What will Antonio say when he is talking about himself?

   Education   I was at ....
   Qualifications I've got ....
   Job   I'm ....
   Hobbies   I like ....
   Future plans   I'd like to become ....

ii) What would *you* say?

B What does he look like?

1 Look at these questions:

Now practise these replies. Which question goes with which reply?

Now use these words in the replies:

Oh yes, very	dark	quite tall	well built
No, not particularly	blond	not very tall	rather thin
	red		rather fat

★ Of course you can ask these questions about women too. But you might get different answers!
   These words are interesting: *Slim* and *well-built* are positive words; it is good to be like this. *Thin* and *fat* are negative words.
   Both men and women can be *good-looking* and *attractive*. Men are *handsome*; women are *pretty* or *beautiful*.

2 Here are the descriptions of some people. Look at the names on the right-hand side. Choose one of them, and tell your partner if it is a man or a woman. Your partner will ask you the questions you have practised. Reply, and he must guess which person you are thinking of.

fair	quite slim	very tall	not particularly good-looking	Robert
	rather thin		very good-looking	Paul
	quite slim	quite tall	not particularly attractive	Helen
	rather thin		very attractive	Jane
	well-built	medium height	not particularly attractive	Sue
	rather fat		fairly attractive	Pauline
dark	rather fat	not very tall	not particularly good-looking	David
	well-built		very good looking	Keith

C Talking about other people

1 On the tape you will hear descriptions of five people. You will hear:

A girl describing her fiancé.
A boy describing a girl he dislikes.
A writer describing a historical figure.
A police description of a criminal.
A friend describing his cousin whom you are going to meet.

i) Listen to the tape. Which person is being described?

ii) Listen again. Fill in as much information as you can.

	Hair	Build	Height	Looks
1 Criminal				
2				
3				
4				
5				

Saying goodbye

 1 i) Listen to the tape. What is happening? Where? When? Do the speakers know each other well? Are they going to see each other again soon? Think about what they might say.

ii) Listen again, and write down what they actually say.

Well, thank you for ....
...., Mr
Wilkinson.

Thanks, and ....
..........................'Bye.

Yes, I ....

That it was a great party, but ....
....

37

Unit 5 Saying goodbye

2 i) In the first dialogue you heard Paul *say he's sorry to leave*. What were his words?
How did James reply?

PAUL: I'm .... I must .... now.
really must be off   ought to leave soon.
have to go soon   time I was off
think about going   really should go

JAMES: Come .... ,
You don't .... already do you?

ii) In the second dialogue, Bob *thanked Mr Wilkinson* for the evening. What did
they say?

BOB: Thank you .... a very .... evening.
a delicious meal   letting us join you
a marvellous time   a great dinner
inviting us   a wonderful party
an entertaining day   giving us such a good time

MR WILKINSON: Thank .... for ....

iii) In the third dialogue, Frank *says he hopes* he'll see Sandra again soon. What did
they say?

FRANK: I'll .... next week, ...?
see you Thursday week
come again soon
keep in touch with me
see you again soon
be back in London soon
meet each other soon

SANDRA: Yes, I hope ....

3 Look at this calendar:

```
                        June
Monday           2    9   16   23   30
Tuesday         (3)  10   17   24
Wednesday        4   11   18   25
Thursday         5   12   19   26
Friday           6   13   20   27
Saturday         7   14   21   28
Sunday      1    8   15   22   29
```

Today is Tuesday, 3 June.

JOHN will see his friend on 11 June. So he says: 'I'll see you Wednesday week'.
Now practise in pairs.

Group A

i) You are these people, and your partner is a friend. Finish the sentences; then say them to your partner.

  1 PETER will see his friend on 19 June. So he says:
     'I'll see you .... fortnight.'

  2 MARY will see her friend on 13 June. So she says:
     'I'll see you Friday ....'

  3 ANNE will see her friend on 20 June. So she says:
     'I'll see you ....'

     MIKE will see his friend on 7 June. So he says:
     'I'll see you this ....'

ii) Now your partner will pretend to be the people below. When are they going to see you again? Listen to what your partner says. In which order is he pretending to be these people? Write a number.

PAULINE will see you on 15 June.
JANET will see you on 3 July.
ALAN will see you on 10 June.
PAUL will see you on 12 June.

Group B

```
              June
Monday        2   9   16  23  30
Tuesday      (3)  10  17  24
Wednesday     4   11  18  25
Thursday      5   12  19  26
Friday        6   13  20  27
Saturday      7   14  21  28
Sunday    1   8   15  22  29
```

i)   Your partner is pretending to be these people. When are they going to see you again? Listen to what your partner says. In which order is he pretending to be these people? Write a number.

ANNE will see you on 20 June.
MARY will see you on 13 June.
MIKE will see you on 7 June.
PETER will see you on 19 June.

ii) You are these people, and your partner is a friend. Finish the sentences, then say them to your partner.

1 PAUL will see his friend on 12 June. So he says:
    'I'll see you a week on ....'

2 PAULINE will see her friend on 15 June. So she says:
    'I'll see you .... Sunday.'

3 ALAN will see his friend on 10 June. So he says:
    'I'll see you in a .... 's time.'

4 JANET will see her friend on 3 July. So she says:
    'I'll see you in a month's ....'

4   You're at a party, and it's time to go home. Your host tries to persuade you to stay. Who says these things? You or your host? How might the sentences finish?

But you've only just ....
Actually, I'm not feeling ....
But it's only 10.00 and ....
I really must. I have to get up ....
But there's still plenty of food ....
Do stay ....
I'm afraid not. Our babysitter ....
I had rather a late night ....
At least stay another ....

Unit 6   Consolidation

A   Interview

Trevor Bottomley is one of the senior administrators of the University of Reading. We talked to him about his work and his background. Here are three sections taken from the interview. Listen to each and answer the questions.

Section 1

1 What is the main topic of conversation here?
2 Now listen in more detail.
   What does Trevor say about:
   students from overseas
   a visit to Nigeria
   his future contacts with students?
3 How is Trevor's job going to change in October?
4 What is the difference between the Senate and the Council of the University?
5 Would you like a job like Trevor's? Would you prefer the one he has now or the one he will have in October? Why?

Section 2

Groupwork

Here Trevor talks about his training for his present job.

1 What sort of training did he have?
2 What developments have taken place in the last twenty years in this area?
3 Did his background help directly in his work?
   What was his educational background?
   What part of England does he come from?

Section 3

Here Trevor talks about the schooling of his children. What does he say? Write a tick:

	Yes	No
1 All his children are still at school.		
2 His daughter is at a Comprehensive school.		
3 Christopher likes French and German.		
4 Comprehensive schools are very unsatisfactory.		
5 Grammar-schools were better than Comprehensives because they were bigger.		

Do you agree with the views put forward here about the size of schools?

B Role-play

Interview your partner. Find out about his job and background. Tell the rest of the class what you learn.

C Grammar to practise

Verb constructions

1

Now reply to these questions using 'may':

Are you going to London?
Is Alan staying for the whole week?
Are you catching the 10.00 train?
Will John have lunch with Anne?
Will you phone the doctor this afternoon?
Will you send her a postcard?
Is Peter going to hire a car?

Are you going to fly back?
Are you going to take the car to the garage?

▶ We can use 'may' to talk about the future when we are not sure what will happen.

2   i)   ⟨ I'D LIKE TO BECOME THE CHIEF ENGINEER. ⟩

What would you like to do?

visit America
fly in Concorde
become rich and famous
understand English jokes
live alone on the top of a mountain

What is your ambition?

WOULD YOU LIKE
ANOTHER DRINK
BEFORE YOU GO?

Your partner is hungry and thirsty. Offer him:

a piece of cake
a sandwich
a glass of beer
a piece of toast
another cup of tea

What food or drink would you like now?

Ask your partner what he'd like to do. Use the ideas in the first part of this exercise.
He must answer 'Yes, I would' or 'No, I wouldn't'.

▶ 'I'd like. . .' is a more polite way of saying 'I want. . .' 'Would you like. . .?' is the
question form.

3

WOULD YOU MIND OPENING YOUR SUITCASE, PLEASE ?

THANK YOU FOR INVITING ME.

Ask people to do these things, then thank them:

fill in this form	show you the way
turn the radio down	take your car to the garage
post a letter for you	buy a ticket for you
close the window	give you a lift

▶ After these constructions, the verb ends in *-ing*. On page 42 there is another construction where the verb ends in *-ing*, this time before the preposition 'to'. Try to find it.

4 JOHN DENNY USED TO STUDY AT MANCHESTER UNIVERSITY.

Make sentences with 'used to', to say these things:

We often got up at 3.00 a.m.	It often rained in summer.
We went to the pictures every night.	I had a different girl friend every night.
In the old days, a pint of beer cost 1p.	I swam across the Channel every night.
I always walked 15 miles to school.	He always got drunk.

DID JOHN DENNY USE TO STUDY AT MANCHESTER UNIVERSITY ?

JOHN DENNY DIDN'T USE TO STUDY AT MANCHESTER UNIVERSITY.

Now make interrogative and negative sentences with 'used to'.

▶ 'Used to' describes a habit in the past. Notice the way questions and negatives are formed, with 'use', and not 'used'. Some people say 'used John Denny to study. . .' and 'John Denny used not to study. . .', but this sounds rather formal and old-fashioned.

Indirect speech constructions

1

Ask about these things:

nearest post office
garage closes
I can buy some stamps
the supermarket opens
the manager will be back

I can post this letter
the last train to London goes
I can get a taxi
the news is on TV

▶ This is a polite way of asking for information. Notice the word order. It's the order used for an ordinary statement, not a question.

2 ⟨HE ASKED ME WHERE THE BUS-STOP FOR READING WAS.⟩

Do exercise 1 again with your partner. Say what he asked you. Begin 'He asked me. . .'

▶ This is the way we report a question. Notice that the word order is the same as in the 'Could you tell me. . .' construction. Also notice the tenses of the verbs: 'asked' and 'was'.

Some other constructions

1 i) ⟨HOW'S MARY?⟩
⟨SHE'S BETTER NOW, THOUGH SHE WAS QUITE ILL RECENTLY.⟩

Practise with your partner. Ask about these people. Reply using 'though':

Peter was in hospital last week.
Kate had a cold recently.
Hilary had to spend last week in bed.
David lost his voice on Tuesday.
You were very worried about Jim yesterday.

ii) ⌇ DID YOU ENJOY YOUR HOLIDAY?

⌇ YES. THE WEATHER WAS TERRIBLE THOUGH.

Say what happened on your holiday. Use 'though':

You got lost on the way to the airport.
It rained every day.
Jon was sick on the plane.
The hotel was only half–built.
You spent too much money.

▶ Notice the two positions in the sentence that the word 'though' can go.

2 i) You don't know anyone else at the party.

Finish these sentences. Use 'any. . . else':

I don't like beer. Do you have. . .?
We go to Italy every year. We never go. . .
John can't come. Can you invite. . .?
We always go to George's Restaurant. We can't go. . .
I only like wine. I don't want. . .

ii) You know someone else at the party.

Finish these sentences. Use 'some. . . else':

I don't like beer. I'd rather have. . .
We go to Italy every year. I'd like to go. . .
John can't come. You'd better invite. . .
We usually go to George's Restaurant. But today I'd rather go. . .
I only like wine, but John wants. . .

▶ 'Something else' means 'some other thing'. The same construction is used with 'someone/somebody' and 'somewhere'. Like all constructions with 'some', there is a similar construction with 'any': 'anything', 'anyone/anybody', 'anywhere'. In general 'some' constructions are used in affirmative sentences, 'any' in negatives and questions.

3

COME IN AND HELP YOURSELF TO SOME FOOD.

Make some sentences using 'self':

Mike had a wash.
Peter and Fred enjoyed the concert.
Peter hit his knee.
Jane cut her hand.
Her two children behaved very well.

▶ There are two reflexive pronouns with 'you': 'yourself' and 'yourselves'. You use 'yourself' when you are speaking about one person. 'Yourselves' is plural, and you use it when you are speaking about more than one person.

4

THEY'LL SEE EACH OTHER NEXT WEEK.

Make some sentences using 'each other':

I'll write to you, and you'll write to me.
John kissed Mary and Mary kissed John.
I've never spoken to Fred, and he's never spoken to me.
Pauline doesn't like Helen and Helen doesn't like Pauline.
Do you love her, and does she love you?

▶ We use 'each other' when we are talking about two people. You *can* also use 'one another' when you are talking about two people, though this is less common. You *must* use 'one another' when you are talking about more than two people.

D Grammar to study

When?

These tables are here to help you understand some important points of English grammar.

  Look at the tables and make sentences from them. Look at the notes with each table and make sure you understand them. Ask your teacher if you need help.

  Then look through the units you have studied. Can you use some of the sentences from the tables in these units?

  You can do this in class or at home.

I Future

	on Thursday / 31 July / Christmas Day
	at 9 o'clock / half past 3 / the weekend *next* Tuesday / week / month *this* afternoon / evening / weekend
	in — 5 minutes / half an hour / a couple of days / a week / a fortnight / a month / 5 minutes' / a week's — time
I'll see you[1] I hope to see you I'm leaving[2] I'm going to leave[3] My plane leaves[4]	Monday week / a week on Monday Tuesday fortnight / a fortnight on Tuesday three weeks on Wednesday
	soon / later tonight / tomorrow / then
	before *after* the play *during*
	before *when* *as soon as* you get back[7] *after*
I won't see you I'm not leaving I'm not going to leave My plane doesn't leave	*until* Thursday / 9 o'clock / tomorrow
I'll stay[5]	*until* Thursday / 9 o'clock / tomorrow
I'll be back[6]	*by* 8 o'clock / Sunday / the end of the month

Notes

1 a) I'll see you on Thursday.   This is the normal, neutral way of talking about the future.

b) He *won't* be able to do it then.	Making a negative with *you/he/she/it/they*.
c) I *won't/shan't* see you on Thursday.	Both are possible for the negative of the neutral future with *I/we*.
d) *Will* you be back before I leave?	Asking a question. Neutral future with *you/he/she/it/they*.
e) *Shall* I come round later?	Question form for *I/we*. Normally making an arrangement or an offer.
f) *Will* I need an umbrella?	Neutral future question for *I/we*. Not an arrangement or an offer.
g) I *must/can/may*, etc., see you on Thursday.	These are all grammatically possible. The meaning depends on the verb used.
2 *I'm leaving* on Thursday.	You are talking about your plans or a definite arrangement. Everything is prepared.
3 a) *I'm going to* leave on Thursday.	You are saying what you (or somebody else) intend to do. (Like 2 but without the idea that arrangements have all been made.)
b) *It's going to* rain tomorrow.	You are saying what you are sure will happen.
4 My plane *leaves* on Thursday.	A timetable. A fixed event.
5 I'll stay *until* Thursday.	Used only with verbs which describe a period of activity or a state of affairs, e.g. sleep, wait, work, stay up, etc. But notice its different use with negatives.
6 I'll be back *by* 8 o'clock.	Something will be completed in the future. This is the latest time. It may happen before then. Only used with verbs that describe an action, e.g. wake up, go to sleep, sit down, arrive, etc.
7 I'm leaving *before he gets* back. My plane leaves *after they arrive*. I'm going to phone *when they arrive*. I'll contact you *as soon as I hear from them*.	Notice the present tense in the second half of the sentence.

II Past

I arrived in England I came to England	*on* Thursday / 31 July / Christmas Day *at* 9 o'clock / half past 3 / the weekend *last* Tuesday / week / weekend *this* morning / afternoon / evening *the next* *the following* morning / afternoon / day *in* the morning / afternoon / evening (*at* night)[1] *during* *before* the war / the Christmas holidays[2] *after* a week / fortnight last Monday a week / fortnight ago (only) recently / yesterday / then *as soon as* I heard the news *before* *after* my uncle died *when* I was 23 *while* the strike was on[3]
I didn't arrive in England	*until* Thursday / 3 days ago / yesterday
I stayed at the party	*until* midnight / everybody had gone[4]
I went into the shop and when I came back	the car had gone[5]

Notes

1 I arrived in England *in the morning*. He left *in the afternoon* and arrived *at night*.	We don't know which morning. cf. 'When I arrived in England it was morning.'
2 a) I arrived *during the war*. b) I arrived *after the beginning of the Christmas holidays* and left *before the New Year*.	*During* is used with something that lasts over a period of time. *Before* and *after* are used with a point in time.
3 I arrived *while* the demonstration was taking place.	The first part describes an action; the second part places it in a context. In the second part, verbs which normally describe an action must be in this tense (past progressive).
4 I *stayed* at the party *until 9 o'clock*.	Only used with verbs describing a state of affairs or a period of activity (see note 5 of table I).
5 When *I came back, the car had gone*.	The context is established in the first part; the second part describes something completed before the time of the first part. Notice the tense (past perfect) in the second part.

III Now

What are you doing?	I'm reading a book *at* the moment / present *this* morning / afternoon / evening / week now / today
What are you interested in?	I'm interested in modern jazz these days / nowadays My present / current interest is modern jazz
What's the date? What date is it?	It's 3 December 1995[1] It's December 3rd 1995[2] 3/12/95[3]

What's the time?
What time is it?
	It's 3 o'clock
	  half past 3
	  quarter past 3
	  3/10/20/25 past 3
	  2/3/4/6, etc., minutes past 3
	
	  quarter to 3
	  5/10/20/25 to 3
	  2/3/4/6, etc., minutes to 3
	
	It's time (for me) to go.
	It's time I left / went home / was off[4]

Notes

1 It's *3 December* 1995	Note the pronunciation: It's *the* third *of* December 1995
2 It's *December 3rd* 1995	Note the pronunciation: It's December *the* third 1995
3 *3/12/95*	Note the pronunciation: *The* third *of* December 1995
4 It's time *I left*	Note the past tense in the second part. This means: I must go now.

Unit 7

Doctors

A Symptoms

1 Practise these:

What questions would the doctor ask?

Practise these questions:

Now practise the statements and questions together.

Think of some more symptoms for common illnesses. What would the doctor ask you if you said you had them?

★ If you feel ill in England, go and see the doctor. If you want to buy drugs from a chemist's shop you normally need a prescription from the doctor. And chemists will not usually advise you about an illness.

B Making an appointment

Before you can go and see the doctor, you must make an appointment. So phone up the receptionist. . .

Practise the dialogue on the left. Then make up a similar dialogue using the words on the right.

Man:	I'd like to make an appointment to see Dr Smith, please.	Man:	Could ....?
Receptionist:	Yes. Your name is?	Receptionist:	Certainly, what's ....?
Man:	My name's. . .	Man:	My name's ....
Receptionist:	How is that spelled?	Receptionist:	How do you ....?
Man:	. . . Is it possible to have an appointment on Friday?	Man:	................Could I ....
Receptionist:	Is 9.45 all right?	Receptionist:	How about ....?
Man:	Yes, that will be fine. Thank you. So that's 9.45 on Friday.	Man:	Friday ....That's ....

★ Most doctors in Britain operate an appointment system. Normally you make an appointment a few days in advance, but if you need to see the doctor urgently, you can usually make an appointment the same day.

C Seeing the doctor

1 You go into the doctor's surgery. Try to complete the dialogue. Use one phrase with each picture.

He asks you what is wrong.   You tell him.

What .... do for you?   I've got ....
.... seems to be .... matter?   I keep getting ....

He asks for details.   You explain.

I see
|When ....?
|How long ....?
|Have you ....?
|Do you ....?

2 What does the doctor say?
Listen to the tape and fill in the blanks

i) Just .... your shirt off, will you. I want to .... to your ....
Thank you. You can .... it on .... now.

ii) Now I want to .... your .... Put this ....
.... under your .... please.

iii) I'm going to .... you an .... Could you .... up
your .... please.

iv) Take this .... to the chemist. He will give you some tablets and
some .... I want you to take 3 .... three .... a
day, and take a .... of the medicine just before you go to
....

v) Go .... and go .... to bed. Keep warm and take things ....
.... for a few days. If you don't feel .... after the ....
come back and see me ....

★ As a visitor to Britain, you can see a doctor free of charge under the National Health Service.

Finding out

 1 i) Listen to the tape. What is happening? Where? When? Do the speakers know each other well? Think about what they might say.

ii) Listen again and write down what they actually say.

Excuse me, I wonder ....

.... what time the

flight from Rome is due, please?

How .... please?

Do you know .... please?

Excuse me, could you tell me if that's

.... please?

2 i) Here are some things you want to find out. Where are you?

When does the film end?   How much does that tape recorder cost?
How long does the concert last?   Has the Munich flight been delayed?
Is the London train running late?   Will you be able to service it today?
How long will the pain last?   How long will it take to mend it?
Did Mary see him smash the window?   Which bus goes to King Street?

  ii) John and Mary want to find out the same things. What do they say?

JOHN: Do you know ....?
MARY: Could you tell me ....?

Which way of asking is the most polite?

3 What do you think these people are asking?

Alan and Jane are going on holiday: Patrick is being interviewed for a job:

What time. . .?   How old. . .?
Excuse me. How long. . .?   How long. . .?
Is it possible. . .?   Why. . .?

Tanya is going shopping with her
mother:

Mummy, where. . .?
When. . .?
How far. . .?

57

4 Groupwork

Group A

Angela works in a tourist information office. So it's her job to give information to people.

i) Imagine *you* are a tourist and your partner is Angela. Ask Angela for information. Write down the answers.

You ask her how much it would cost to go by taxi from the centre of London to Heathrow airport.

You want to know how to get to Piccadilly Circus.

You are trying to find out whether you can phone direct to Japan without speaking to the operator.

You would like to know whether there are any food shops open in London in the evenings.

ii) Now *you* are Angela and your partner is a tourist. Give him the information he asks for.

It is possible to hire a car in London and leave it at Dover. Don't forget we drive on the left.

You do have to pay for an appointment at an English dentist. How much you pay depends on the treatment you have.

Usually people leave a 10% tip to the waiter in London restaurants. Don't leave any more.

The National Gallery is open on Sundays. Get there early, before the crowds.

Group B

Angela works in a tourist information office. So it's her job to give information to people.

i) Imagine *you* are Angela and your partner is a tourist. Give him the information he asks for.

   If you wish to telephone Japan, you must book the call through the operator. It is not possible to dial direct. Ask for the international operator.

   The taxi fare from the centre of London to Heathrow is about £10. Don't pay more than this.

   There are a few food shops open in London in the evenings. There's one in Chelsea. Get there before 10.00.

   It's easy to get to Piccadilly Circus. Take a tube from Green Park. Don't get on the wrong tube.

ii) Now *you* are a tourist and your partner is Angela. Ask Angela for information. Write down the answers.

   You ask whether the National Gallery is open on Sundays.

   You want to know whether you usually leave tips in London restaurants.

   You have toothache. You want to know whether you have to pay at the dentists in England.

   You would like to know whether you can hire a car in London and leave it in Dover.

5 i) Here are some answers. What were the questions? When your partner asks a
question, give him the answer.

It takes about half an hour by car.
It costs £2.30 for three minutes.
10 o'clock, I think.
Yes, it's 386 5100.
It's an American group – the Eagles I think.
It leaves at 13.28.
It should be in at the end of next week.
It's Mr Smith's I think.

ii) Ask the same questions again in a different way.
Your partner will give you the answer.

Unit 8

Telephones

A On the phone

1 Practise these. Who says these things? When?

HELLO, 369 7482

DIRECTORY ENQUIRIES. FOR WHICH TOWN, PLEASE?

COULD I LEAVE A MESSAGE FOR HER, PLEASE?

HELLO, COULD I SPEAK TO ANDREW, PLEASE?

I'M AFRAID THE LINE IS ENGAGED, CALLER.

How would you reply?

Practise these replies:

OH, I'M TERRIBLY SORRY. I'VE GOT THE WRONG NUMBER.

FOR MANCHESTER, PLEASE.

I'M AFRAID HE'S NOT HERE AT THE MOMENT.

THANK YOU OPERATOR. I'LL TRY AGAIN LATER

JUST A MINUTE AND I'LL GET HIM. WHO'S CALLING?

YES OF COURSE. JUST WAIT A MINUTE AND I'LL GET A PEN.

Now practise these sentences together.

★ When you answer the phone in Britain, you start by giving your number. Notice how the numbers are pronounced, e.g. 85123 = eight five one two three. There are only two problems: 0 is normally pronounced *oh*, e.g. 5049 = five oh four nine; and a number like 332441 is normally pronounced double three two double four one. If you don't know the number of the person you want to phone, you can look in the directory. Most phones have a directory for the area. If you want a number in another part of the country, dial 192 and Directory Enquiries will give you the number. In an emergency, dial 999 anywhere in the country and you will be connected to the Fire Brigade, Police or Ambulance service.

2   What would you say?

i)

You want to ring up a friend who lives in Southampton. You don't know the code to dial so you decide to ask the operator. You dial 100 and she answers.

Hello could you. . .?'

You want to phone up some more friends who live in:

Edinburgh	Sidcup
Cardiff	Leicester
Reading	Oxford

any more?

ii)

GOOD MORNING, RICHARDS LTD.

You want to talk to the manager of a large company. So you dial the number of the company and the switchboard operator answers. You know that his extension number is 7673.

'Hello, I'd like. . .'

You want to talk to some other people in the company. Their extension numbers are:

832	5832
749	4422
8620	3022

any more?

iii)

You want to phone up a friend who lives in Beccles. You know that his number is Beccles 3289 but you want the operator to get the number for you. You dial 100 and the operator answers.

'Hello, could I have. . .?'

You want to phone up some more friends. Their numbers are:

Cambridge 22487   01 382 7674
Banbury 3476   061 483 3004
St Helens 24188   021 623 8244   any more?

iv)

You answer the phone. Someone wants to speak to your flat-mate David, but he is out.

'Sorry, I'm afraid he's not in. Can I. . .?'

★ Most towns in Britain now have an STD code beginning with 0, e.g. 01 = London, 0734 = Reading. If you use this code you can dial straight to these towns without going through the operator. This is quicker and cheaper. Calls through the operator are much more expensive than calls you dial yourself.

B Still on the phone!

1 Listen to these dialogues on the tape. Here are some phrases from the tape but some words are missing. Write down the words from the tape.

i)

– Oh I'm sorry. I've got the .... I'm terribly sorry.
– Could I speak to Mr Thompson, please? Extension .... I think.
– Could I .... Peter Thompson please?
– I'm sorry. He's not here at the moment. Can I take a ....?
– Could you tell him that Tony .... and ask him to ....
    ....? He knows the number.

ii)

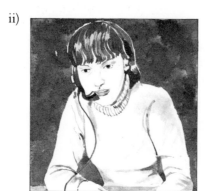

– Grantham 3422. You can .... that yourself you know, if you use the
    STD ....
– What is your exchange and .... please?
– Right. Could you have .... please.
– I'm sorry caller. The line's ....
– O.K., cancel the call, please. I'll .... later.

★ The cost of a phone call in Britain depends on the time of day you make it. The cheapest time is between 6 p.m. and 8 a.m. – or any time at weekends. The most expensive time is between 9 a.m. and 1 p.m. on weekdays.

iii)

– You'll have to phone Directory ....
– Yes, I suppose so. .... isn't it?
– Directory Enquiries. For .... please?
– And the .... please?
– Here is the number. It's Ipswich ....

2   Now use the words you have practised.

i)   try to phone up:

Paul Johnson Ext. 834   Helen Ritchie Ext. 3982
Derek Albott Ext. 7842   Jane Campbell Ext. 6843
Peter Jukes Ext. 359   Carola Robinson Ext. 224

ii) Ask Directory Enquiries for the numbers of some people you know in Britain. If
     you do not know any details (name of town, name of person, address), make
     them up.

★   It is not normally possible to make phone calls from pubs and cafes in Britain. But there are plenty of
    public phone boxes on the streets, as well as at stations, and airports. You pay for these calls with 2p and
    10p coins.
       You can also dial direct to many countries overseas. Dial 010 for the international service, and then
    the code for the country and town you want. Full details are in the STD code booklet. This is usually
    cheaper in the evenings – after 8 p.m.

Asking people to do things

 1 i) Listen to the tape. What is happening? Where? When? Do the speakers know each other well? What kind of favours are they asking? Think about what they might say.

ii) Listen again and write down what they actually say.

Could I possibly ....
.........................?

You couldn't ....
...., could you?

Could you ....
.... for me, please?

Look, ...
.... will you, dear?

66

2   Look at these situations. How do Alan, John, Mike and Tony ask others to do things for them? Try to complete the sentences:

i)

Alan wants to make a phone call. He hasn't got any change.

What would he say if he wanted someone to:

open the window   close the door   check the oil

explain a word   answer the phone   translate a letter

ii)

John wants to order some wine.

What would he say if he wanted:

| another cognac | a timetable | another appointment |
| some leaflets | the international operator | the recipe |

Where would he ask for these things?

iii)

Mike wants to buy a car, but hasn't got enough money. So he asks his father.

What would he say if he wanted his father to:

take him to the airport
do some shopping for him
lend him the car
look after his baby for the day
help him paint the house

iv)

Tony wants a newspaper. His wife is going to the shops.

What would he say if he wanted his wife to:

turn the kettle off
put the car in the garage
lend him £5
turn the radio down
pass the salt
open the wine

3 i) Can you help? Look at these conversations:

SANDRA: Could you change this £1 note for me, please?
CASHIER: Yes, I think so.
SANDRA: Thank you very much.

ANDREW: Could I have a timetable, please?
CLERK: I'm sorry. I'm afraid not. We haven't got any left.
ANDREW: Oh, I see. Well, thank you anyway.

ii) Here are some situations you saw in the last exercise. Choose six of them, and think of reasons for saying no.

Alan wants someone to:	John wants:
open the window	another cognac
answer the phone	the international operator
explain a word	some leaflets
check the oil	another appointment
close the door	a timetable
translate a letter	the recipe

Practise the conversations.

4 i) Who says these things? In what situations?

a) It would help if you could hold the torch for me a second and I'll see if I can find it.	Hold ....?
b) I wonder if you could move your head a little. I can't see.	Could you ....?
c) I want you to run round and tell John to come back home immediately.	Run ....?
d) As it's raining, I thought you might collect him by car.	You couldn't ....?
e) What *is* the time? Mine's stopped.	Could you ....?
f) I like it better over there. Do me a favour and move it for me, dear.	Move ....?
g) I wonder if you could change it. I like to have a clean tablecloth.	You couldn't ....?
h) Let me borrow yours, George. I've only got a pencil.	Could I ....?

ii) Make new sentences using the words on the right.

iii) How do you think the other person replies? They don't say yes all the time. Maybe they can't help.

Unit 9

Garages

A Saying what is wrong

1 Practise these:

What do you think the mechanic might reply?

Practise these replies:

Now practise the statements and replies together.

2 What would you say? How would you tell the mechanic what is wrong?

i)

'.................... don't work.'

It's getting dark and you want to put on the headlights. But when you press the switch, nothing happens.

Now the same thing happens with:

the sidelights
the horn
the radio
the direction indicator
the heater
the windscreen wipers

ii)

'There's something wrong ....'

You notice that the brakes don't work properly, so you take the car straight to the garage.

Now the same thing happens with:

the direction indicators
the brake lights
the petrol pump
the exhaust system
the speedometer
the fuel gauge

iii)

'The engine keeps................'

You are driving along when the engine suddenly stops. You start it again, but a few minutes later the same thing happens. And then it happens again.

Here are some more things that keep happening:

The mirror falls off every ten minutes.
The sidelights go out five times in half an hour.
The door opens when you're driving along.
The front seat moves forward every time you stop.
Whenever you touch the brakes, the horn sounds.

★ There are two motoring organisations that help motorists in trouble – the Automobile Association (AA) and the Royal Automobile Club (RAC). Your own national motoring association is probably affiliated to one of these.
  If you break down on a motorway you can phone for help from one of the phone boxes found there. There is one every mile.

3   Talking to the mechanic.

Your car has broken down in the main street. You walk to the nearest garage and talk to the mechanic. Try to complete the dialogue. Use one phrase with each picture.

You go up to the mechanic. What does he say?

Hello, ... I do for you?
Hello, ... I help you?

You explain what is wrong

There's a terrible ....
The battery ....
I've got ....

What does he reply?

Well don't worry. We'll ....
I'll have a look ....

You tell him where the car is.

Thank you. It's ....

4 Listen to the tape and write down some of the words you hear.

– I've .... petrol. You couldn't .... some out to me, could
you?

– Just .... Chome on the road to Winton. Just .... the junction
with the Hamford road.

– It's a Morris 1100 – a blue one. .... number KFN 396M.

– Well, could you possibly bring five .... with you? I'll put the
.... up so that you'll see me.

B Buying petrol

1

Look at these instructions for a self-service petrol pump. They are in the wrong order. Can you sort them out.

Place nozzle in petrol tank
Replace nozzle in holster
Press yellow button to select grade of petrol
Check display and pay cashier
Squeeze trigger until required amount is indicated

2 £5 WORTH OF 3-STAR, PLEASE.

FOUR GALLONS OF 2-STAR, PLEASE.

FILL IT UP WITH 3-STAR, PLEASE.

Now you ask for petrol:

3-star – £3   5-star – three gallons
2-star – fill   3-star – fill
4-star – five gallons   4-star – £5
3-star – £4   2-star – £4

★ Self-service filling stations are becoming very popular in Britain. Petrol is often cheaper at these stations. You buy petrol either by quantity or by price.
    There are different grades of petrol: 5-star is very high quality and is used in sports cars and others with high performance engines. Most cars need 4-star or 3-star. Some modern cars are specially designed to use 2-star petrol, which is the cheapest.
    While you're at the petrol station you can also check the oil in your engine, and the tyre pressures.

Asking for permission

 1 i) Listen to the tape. What is happening? Where? When? Do the speakers know each other well? Think about what they might say.

ii) Listen again and write down what they actually say.

I'd like to .... Does anybody mind?

Could I possibly ....
.... ?

Do you mind if ....
.... ?

You don't mind if ....
.... ?

75

2 i) You have rented a room in Mrs Armstrong's house. Here are some things that you want to do. To be polite, you ask Mrs Armstrong first. You say. . .

Could I possibly have a TV in my room?
Could I possibly put some pictures on the walls?
Could I possibly ask some friends to call round on Sunday?
Could I possibly get another front door key?
Could I possibly put my bicycle in the garage?
Could I possibly come back late on Saturday?
Could I possibly paint my bedroom?
Could I possibly move the furniture in my room?
Could I possibly use the washing machine?
Could I possibly dry my clothes on the line?

Now ask her permission in three other ways.

I'd like to. . .
You don't mind if. . .
Do you mind if. . .

ii) Here are some reasons Mrs Armstrong might give for saying no. Which questions is she replying to?

You might damage the walls.
My relations are coming on Sunday.
You might wake the children when you come in.
We like it where it is.
You can watch our TV if you want to.
It's dangerous to have too many copies.
I'm doing my own drying today.
I like it the colour it is.
It's broken down.
You might scratch my husband's car.

3 Look at these conversations:

SALLY: You don't mind if I use your hairdryer, do you?
ANGELA: No, of course not. It's in the cupboard.
TERRY: Do you mind if I use your hammer?
BERNARD: I'm sorry. I'm afraid I haven't got one.

Where would you keep these things? (Look at the list of likely places on the next page.)

hairdryer   record player
pen   bottle opener
umbrella   bicycle
screwdriver
tie

In the . . .

wardrobe?	desk?
garage?	tool box?
kitchen?	sitting room?
bedroom?	

Choose four of these things. If your partner asks to borrow them, say yes and tell him where they are. If he asks to borrow anything else, say no and give a reason.

4 Groupwork

Group A

Mr Palmer is the manager of a small private company. His employees are always coming to ask his permission to do things.

i) Imagine *you* work for Mr Palmer. Ask his permission. Does he say yes or no?

You want to take next Tuesday off to go and visit a sick relative in Oxford.

YES/NO

You'd like an advance in salary. You want to buy a car this month.

YES/NO

You want to change offices. Your present one is too noisy.

YES/NO

You want to borrow the company car to collect some things from town.

YES/NO

ii) Now you are Mr Palmer.

You don't need to use your calculator today.

An important visitor is coming tomorrow at 9.15. Everybody must be in the office.

There's not much to do in the office next week. So staff can take holidays if they wish.

There's no extra evening work to do this week.

Group B

Mr Palmer is the manager of a small private company. His employees are always coming to ask his permission to do things.

i) You are Mr Palmer. When your partner asks your permission will you say yes or no?

No one can have an advance in salary this month.

The company car is free, but it must be back by 2 o'clock.

No one can change offices. There are no other offices free.

You always allow people to take time off when a relative is ill.

ii) Now you work for Mr Palmer. Ask his permission. Does he say yes or no?

You want to work late this week. You need the extra money.

YES/NO

You'd like to arrrive late tomorrow. You have a dental appointment at 9.00.

YES/NO

You'd like permission to use Mr Palmer's calculator. You have some complicated figures to work out.

YES/NO

Your're moving house next week, and you want to take the week off work.

YES/NO

5   i)   What can you ask your partner's permission about? He must give or refuse
          permission using one of the sentences.

          It's in the cupboard over there.
          It's broken I'm afraid.

          There's an ashtray over there.
          Cigarette smoke makes me sick.

          I don't want to wake up the children.
          I can't hear it very well either.

          I've got a terrible cold and I mustn't sit in a draught.
          It's awfully hot in here isn't it?

     ii) Now your partner will ask permission about the same things in a different way.
          Give or refuse it using one of the sentences given.

Unit 10

Shops

A In the shop

1 Practise these:

How would you reply?

Practise these replies

Now practise the questions and replies together.

★ Many shops and stores in Britain do not accept travellers cheques, but more and more places accept credit cards. If you have a credit card in your own country you may be able to use it in Britain – but check with your bank about currency regulations.

B   Which shop?

1   Which shops would you go to to buy these things?

Shopping List

cigarettes   razor blades
air-mail letter   chocolates
  beer   shampoo
      stamps   postal order
red wine   aspirin
      matches   lemonade.

2   Now ask for things using the words in this table:

	a can of	Stinkos special filter	
	a £3	matches	
	a packet of	milk chocolates	
	a small box of	air mail letters	
Can I have	20·	stamps	please?
	a bottle of	postal order	
	a sachet of	aspirin	
	3	shampoo	
	half a dozen 10p	razor blades	
		beer	
		red wine	
		lemonade	

Think of some more shops. What could you buy there? Practise asking for them.

C Buying things

1 i) Listen to the dialogue on the tape and fill in the blanks.

SHOP ASSISTANT: Can I .... you?
CUSTOMER: Yes, I'm looking for a ....
SHOP ASSISTANT: What .... did you want?
CUSTOMER: I think I need a size ....
SHOP ASSISTANT: Here you .... look.
CUSTOMER: Yes, that's nice. How .... is it?

SHOP ASSISTANT: This one costs .... I think. Would you like to .... it
one?
[Pause]
Does it .... ?
CUSTOMER: Yes, it's fine. I'll .... it.

ii) Practise this dialogue in pairs.

2 Make up some new dialogues in a boutique or a shoe shop.

SIZES

WOMEN'S CLOTHES							
British	10	12	14	16	18	20	
Continental	38	40	42	44	46	48	
SHOES							
British	3	4	5	6	7	8	9	10
Continental	36	37	38	39	41	42	43	44

★ Men's clothes do not have standard sizes like women's. Shirts are sold according to the size of the collar;
14 is small, 15 medium and 16 large. Sweaters, etc., are sold according to the chest measurement. Often
this is expressed in inches although metric sizes are being introduced; 36 is small, 40 medium, and 44
large. Trousers depend on the waist measurement, and the length of the inside leg. For the waist, 30 is
small, 34 medium and 38 large; for the leg 26 is short, 30 is medium and 34 is tall.

D Complaining

1 Practise these:

2 What happens when you take these things back?

Saying thank you

1 i) Listen to the tape. What is happening? Where? When? Do the speakers know each other well? Think about what they might say?

   ii) Listen again and write down what they actually say.

Well, thanks .... us.

Thank you very much indeed for your ....

It really is good of you to ....showing me around.

I would have .... otherwise.

84

2   You're waiting at the bus stop and your friend drives past. He stops and gives you a lift. . .

Now practise thanking these people in two ways:

a) You've left your pen at home and Mike has lent you his.
b) You've never used the phone before in England, and Sheila has helped you make a call.
c) You thought your friend David had forgotten your birthday, but then he gives you a present.
d) You've missed the last bus home and Anne and Tony are letting you stay at their house.
e) Paul's having a party on Saturday, and he's just invited you.
f) You're feeling rather sick, and are having a day in bed. Linda has done the shopping for you.
g) You want to buy a car, and Mike who knows all about cars, has just given you some advice.
h) You're in hospital and feeling miserable. Andrew has come to visit you.
i) Your own car has broken down, and Arthur has let you use his.

3 i) Sometimes when you thank people, you also say what would (or wouldn't) have happened if they hadn't helped you.

I	would / wouldn't	have	caught the train / run out of food / seen her / had an accident / got a ticket / got lost	otherwise.

Here are six situations. Thank people and say what would or wouldn't have happened:

a) John has told you how to get to the shopping centre.
b) Linda has booked you a seat for a concert.
c) Two friends have helped you take a heavy suitcase upstairs.
d) You want to speak to Jane, and Harry has told her this.
e) Mary has given you a lift to the station.
f) It's Friday evening, and you have forgotten to go to the bank. Alan has lent you some money.

ii) When would you say these sentences? What could you be thanking the other person for? Practise thanking:

I would have got the wrong train otherwise.
I would have got very wet otherwise.
I wouldn't have finished in time otherwise.
I would have been a bit lonely otherwise.
I wouldn't have passed the exam otherwise.
I wouldn't have known which number to ring otherwise.

4 In each of these sentences someone is being thanked. But for what? In what situations?

a) That's very kind of you. I left my wallet at home.
b) Very many thanks. I didn't want to walk home.
c) Many thanks indeed. It was rather cold in here.
d) It really is good of you. Shakespeare's my favourite.
e) You're very kind. Mine's broken down.
f) Thanks a lot. Mine's still at the cleaners.
g) I appreciate the help. I've never changed a tyre in my life.
h) You really shouldn't have. It's what I always wanted.

Now make new sentences like this:

'Thanks for lending me the money. I left my wallet at home.'

Unit 11 Consolidation

A Interview

Dr Gunn is the Director of the Health Centre at a British university. We talked to Dr Gunn about his work and his background and we have taken three sections from what he said for you to listen to.

Section 1

1 What is the main topic of conversation here?
2 Now listen in more detail. What does Dr Gunn say about:
   studying languages
   Egyptian hieroglyphics
   the University of Manchester?
3 What general advantage has his non-medical background been to Dr Gunn? Does he give any concrete examples?
4 How many jobs has Dr Gunn had since he qualified? Where does he work now?
5 What did a retired watchmaker, a dentist and Dr Gunn have in common? What is the expression Dr Gunn uses to describe them?

Section 2

Groupwork

In this section, Dr Gunn talks about changes in the role of a doctor.
The main changes are, he feels, technological. What examples of this does he give?
He also mentions a change in the personal relationship between doctor and patient.
How has the relationship changed?
What does Dr Gunn say is the next stage in the development of medicine?

Section 3

In this section, Dr Gunn talks about the future of private medicine and its effect on the National Health Service. What does he think? Write a tick ✓:

	Yes	No	Don't know
1 There are now very few opportunities for private care in NHS hospitals.			
2 There will be an explosion in the growth of private medicine.			

87

	Yes	No	Don't know
3 Private hospital treatment is not very expensive.			
4 The cost of private medicine is going up every year.			
5 Private medicine will develop alongside the NHS.			

B Role-play

You work for an insurance company which runs a private medical scheme.
Mr Williams is a businessman who wants to join your scheme. What questions will you ask him when he comes to your office? Will you accept him for your scheme?

C Grammar to practise

Verb constructions

1

THE ENGINE KEEPS STOPPING.

Make some more sentences using 'keep':

Sue and Sylvia always talk when you're trying to work.
Paul always borrows your pencil.
The dog next door always barks at night.
Your teacher always gives you too much homework.
David and Robin always arrive late.
You and your friend always lose your way.
Your partner always falls asleep during the lesson.
Anne always asks stupid questions.
That cat always sits on your coat.

Think of some things which people do and which annoy you. Make sentences using 'keep'.

▶ We use 'keep' for actions that happen very frequently. It often gives the idea that you are a little angry.

2

IT'S GOOD OF YOU TO SHOW ME ROUND.

I'M GRATEFUL TO YOU FOR GIVING ME A LIFT.

Say thank you to these people:

Mark gave you a lift.
Martin and Jillian translated the letter for you.
Gloria did your shopping for you.
Eddy lent you a book.
Mike got you a taxi.
Cathy helped you wash up.
Tim let you stay in his house.
John carried your heavy suitcase.

Now tell someone else how grateful you are to these people. Like this:

IT'S GOOD OF JOHN TO GIVE ME A LIFT.

I'M GRATEFUL TO JOHN FOR GIVING ME A LIFT.

▶   Notice that 'good of. . .' is followed by the infinitive with 'to', and 'grateful to. . .' is followed by 'for' and the verb in *-ing*.

3

IF YOU DON'T FEEL BETTER, COME BACK AND SEE ME.

How would you advise these people?

If you want to know the time. . .
If it rains. . .
If you don't like walking. . .
If you want to speak good English. . .
If you like good food. . .

And these people?

Jon can never get up in the morning.
Keith can never do any work in his house.
Moyra doesn't like travelling by plane.
George wants to be rich.
Alice wants to be an actress.

▶   You can also use this construction with the negative imperative 'If you feel ill, don't go out of the house'.

4

IT'S BROKEN DOWN.

Do you know what these expressions mean:

give up   drop in
stand out   calm down
turn round   break down

Use the expressions to finish these sentences:

Someone tapped him on the shoulder. He ....
Everyone was wearing red except Mary. She ....
Margaret was excited when she passed her exams. Then she ....
Paul's car was very old. It kept ....
Sally and Sue were shopping near our house. They ....

▶ Notice that these verbs cannot be followed by a noun.

5

JOHN IS GOING TO FALL OVER THE CAT.
HE'S FALLEN OVER.

Make sentences like the second one.

Mary and Sam are going to come into the room.
Janet is going to sit down on the chair.
Susan is going to drive past your house.
The diver is going to go under the water.
The key is going to fall out of her purse.

▶ Notice that these verbs can be followed by a noun, but do not have to be.

Indirect speech constructions

> COULD YOU TELL ME HOW TO GET TO
> PICCADILLY CIRCUS ?

> COULD YOU TELL ME WHICH BUS GOES TO
> KING STREET ?

> COULD YOU TELL ME WHEN THE FILM ENDS?

Ask these questions using 'could':

How do I work this machine?
How do I fill in this form?
How do I get from London to Oxford?
How do I make a telephone call to Germany?
How do I open a bank account?
Which pen is yours?
Which road should I take?
Which train stops in Manchester?
Which day is he coming?
Which terminal should I go to?

Here are some more questions to ask using 'could':

When does the bus leave?
How much is the fare?
What do you want to buy?
How many people will be coming?
Where do you live?
What's your nationality?
What time will you be home?
Who asked you to come here?

▶ In unit 6 you saw 'could you tell me. . .' followed by 'where'. In this exercise you have practised the same construction followed by other question words, like 'how', 'which' and 'what'.
   Notice that the word order is the same as for an ordinary statement, not a question.

Some other constructions

Reply to these questions using 'really' and 'very much', like this:

A: Do you like fast cars?
B: Yes, I really like them.
   Yes, I like them very much.

Did you like the film?
Do you want to see him?
Are you enjoying the holiday?
Are you looking forward to Christmas?
Would you like to speak English well?
Do you like England?

▶ You *can* put 'very much' before the verb if you wish – 'yes, I very much like them', but this is not so common.
You *cannot* put 'really' after the main verb.

Now reply to the same questions, like this:

A: Do you like fast cars?
B: Yes, I really do.
   Yes, I do, very much.

▶ In this sort of sentence, where an auxiliary like 'do' replaces a main verb, like 'want', you *cannot* put 'very much' before the auxiliary.

D Grammar to study

How long?

These tables are here to help you to understand some important points of English grammar.

Look at the tables and make sentences from them. Look at the notes with each table and make sure you understand them. Ask your teacher if you need help.

Then look through the units you have studied. Can you use some of the sentences from the tables in these units?

You can do this in class or at home.

I In the past, completed

He stayed in London[1]	*for* three days / a week / six months[2] *over* the summer / the weekend / Christmas[3] *all* winter / weekend / day[4] *from* May *to* / *until* October[5] *until* 1970 / 3 May / last Tuesday (*for*) a long time / ages (*for*) a while / a short time temporarily
Did he stay in London He didn't stay in London	long[6]

Notes

1 He *stayed* in London	Notice the past tense. Here we are talking about things which are now finished.
2 *for*	is used to express the length of a period of time. Sometimes *for* is not necessary, but it can normally be used in expressions like this.
3 *over*	is used with a definite, named period of time, e.g. the summer, the winter, the weekend, Easter.
4 *all*	notice that *for* is never used with *all*.
5 *from/until*	these are both used to define a point in time, e.g. 10 o'clock; Tuesday; yesterday; 12 May; 1975. A period of time starts at the point defined by *from* and ends at the point defined by *to/until*.
6 *long*	notice that this is used only with questions and negatives. We don't use *for* or *a long time* in questions or negatives.

93

II   Starting in the past, lasting until now

He has been in London[1] It has been snowing[2]	*for* three days / a week / six months[3] *all* winter / weekend / day *since* yesterday / last week / Nov 3rd[4] (for) a long time / ages (for a while / a short time
Has he been in London He hasn't been in London Has it been snowing It hasn't been snowing	long

Notes

1 He *has been* in London	Notice the present perfect tense (*not* the present). We are talking about a situation which still exists. He is still in London.
2 It *has been snowing*	Notice the present perfect progressive tense. Action verbs are normally used in this tense, to emphasise that the action has been in progress up to now.
3 *for*	is used exactly as in table I – to express the length of a period of time.
4 *since*	is used to define a point in time when something started (cf. *from* in table I), e.g. since 10 o'clock; Tuesday; yesterday; 1975. Here the thing that started then is still continuing.

III   In the future

I'm staying in London I'll stay in London I'm going to stay in London	*for* three days / a week / six months *over* the summer / the weekend / Christmas *all* winter / weekend / day *from* May *to* / *until* October *until* the end of next month (*for*) a long time / ages (*for*) a while / a short time temporarily
Are you staying in London I'm not staying in London I won't stay in London I'm not going to stay in London	long

Notes

For notes on the expressions used here, see table I.
For notes on the different ways of referring to the future, see unit 6, table I.

IV   Three useful verbs

I *spent* three weeks studying this problem. Then I found the answer.
I *have spent* a long time looking for a house I can afford. I'm still looking.
I'm *going to spend* my holidays at home next year.

The journey *lasted* six and a half hours. Thank goodness it's over.
The film *has lasted* six hours already. I want to go home.
The concert *will last* until 10.30.

It *took* three hours to get from the airport to the city centre.
It *has taken* me three weeks – and I still haven't finished the book.
The journey is *going to take* at least ten hours.

Unit 12

Travelling

A Taxis

1 Practise these:

How might the driver reply?

Practise these replies:

Now practise what the passenger says and what the driver replies together.

★ You will find taxis at all airports and large stations. In large towns there are also taxi ranks in the streets, and in London and some other towns taxis drive round the streets looking for customers.

A word of warning. If you arrive at London Airport and take a taxi to the city centre, it will be very expensive. It is much better to take a coach or catch the tube. Your airline will give you more details.

2 On the tape you will hear someone booking a taxi. Listen to the tape and fill in the blanks.

– I'd like to .... a taxi please.

– I have to be at the station .... half past seven.

– I'm sorry. We're completely .... then. We've nothing ....
until 9 o'clock.

– Oh well, I'd better .... then.

– I see. Where .... from?

– So we'll have to .... you up about 7 o'clock.

– Just a minute. What was the .... again?

3 TAXI DRIVER: Where shall I drop you?

PASSENGER: Opposite. . .

In front of. . . please

Behind. . .

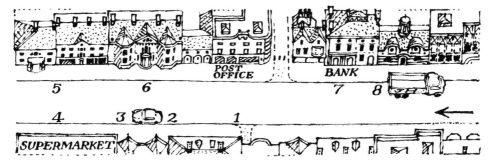

4 What is the fare?

Student A	*Student B*
Ask your partner and write down what he says.	Make up some fares, write them down and tell your partner.
How much do I owe you?	That's 80p please

1	6	1	6 ....
2	7	2	7 ....
3	8	3	8 ....
4	9	4	9 ....
5	10	5	10 ....

★ The price you pay for a taxi is shown on a meter (the clock) at the end of the journey. There is always a minimum charge, and you normally add about 10% tip for the driver.

B Buses

1 Practise these questions:

What might the woman reply?

Practise these replies:

Now practise the questions and replies together.

★ There are some bus stops at which buses must stop, and others – called 'request stops' – where buses only stop if you signal to them by holding out your arm. Request stops are marked, but if you are in any doubt it is best to signal the bus you want.

2   Finding out about buses

Group A

Practise finding out which bus you want, and when the next one is due.
Imagine your partner is a passer-by. Ask him for information and write down what
he says.

a)   You are at the Car Park. You want to go to the Gaumont Cinema. It is 2.50.
     Bus Number ....   Time of next bus ....

b)   You are at the Town Hall. You want to go to the Football Stadium. It is 6.35.
     Bus number ....   Time of next bus ....

c)   You are at the Zoo. You want to go to the University. It is 7.40.
     Bus number ....   Time of next bus ....

d)   You are at the Car Park. You want to go to the Swimming Baths. It is 3.25.
     Bus number ....   Time of next bus ....

e)   You are at the Hospital. You want to go to the University. It is 7.55.
     Bus number ....   Time of next bus ....

Group B

You are a passer-by and your partner asks you for some information. Look at the
timetables and answer your partner's questions.

a)   You are at the Car Park. It is 2.50.   d)   You are at the Car Park. It is 3.25.
b)   You are at the Town Hall. It is 6.35.   e)   You are at the Hospital. It is 7.55.
c)   You are at the Zoo. It is 7.40.

Service No 15. Winton Car Park → New Theatre → Swimming Baths → Gaumont Cinema

Car Park	2.15	2.30	2.45	3.00	3.15	3.30	3.45	4.00	4.15	4.30	4.45	5.0
New Theatre	2.25	2.40	2.55	3.10	3.25	3.40	3.55	4.10				
Swimming Baths	2.35	2.50	3.05	3.20	3.35	3.5						
Gaumont Cinema	2.45	3.00	3.15	3.30	3.4							

Service No 26.   Town Hall → New Theatre → Football Stadium

Town Hall	3.00	4.00	5.00	6.00	7.00	8.00	9.00
New Theatre	3.15	4.15	5.15	6.15	7.15	8.15	
Football Stadium	3.25	4.25	5.25	6.25	7.25		

Service No 49.   Hospital → Zoo → University

Hospital	7.00	7.20	7.40	8.00	8.20	8.40	9.00
Zoo	7.15	7.35	7.55	8.15	8.35	8.55	
University	7.25	7.45	8.05	8.25	8.4		

★   Nowadays many buses in Britain do not have conductors – only drivers, so you must pay the driver the
money for your fare when you get on. Keep the ticket he gives you because it may be checked by an
inspector.

3 Practise asking where the bus stop is:

Group A: Ask about No. 15, No. 28, No. 181, No. 52, No. 22.
Group B: Ask about No. 26, No. 14, No. 49, No. 42, No. 20.
When you are asking, look only at the first map, and write the numbers in the correct box.

Give the information from the second map.

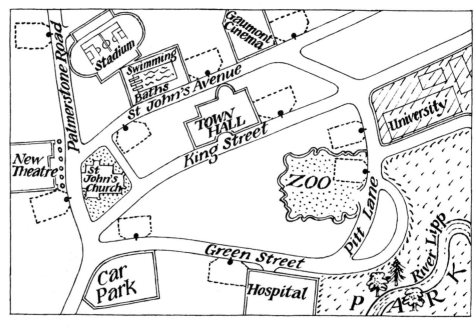

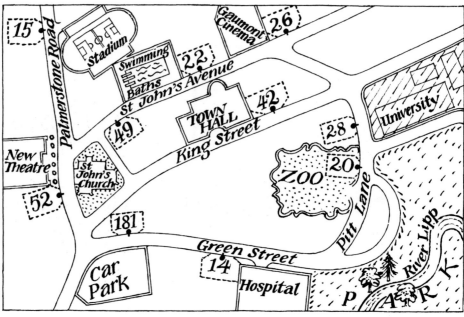

Inviting and suggesting

 1 i) Listen to the tape. What is happening? Where? When? Do the speakers know each other well? Think about what they might say.

ii) Listen again and write down what they actually say.

Listen Gary. Would you like ....?

Let's go and ....

Well, I'll tell you what. Why not .... ?

How about .... ?

2   On the tape you heard people using different ways of inviting and suggesting. What were they? Complete the following sentences:

i)   .... to come round to dinner on Friday?

go / football match / Saturday
go and hear / piano recital / concert hall
see / play / theatre / next week
watch / tennis tournament / university

ii)   .... and see that horror film on at the Odeon.

go / London / weekend
go and see / exhibition / library
meet / pub / after work
have tea together / Tuesday

iii)   .... sleep at our house?

open / bank account
look it up / phone book
take it back / shop
find / baby-sitter

iv)   .... going for a walk by the river'

hire a car / weekend
take / day off
do / washing up / tomorrow
buy us all / drink

3   i)   Practise inviting and suggesting, like David, Frank, Pauline, Vera:

DAVID: Would you like to. . .?   PAULINE: Let's. . .
FRANK: Why not. . .?   VERA: How about. . .?

John's party	Wednesday
the dance	Sunday
lunch together	Friday
the museum	Monday
a drive in the country	Tuesday
the cricket match	Saturday
the zoo in London	Thursday

ii)   Now work in pairs. Write down what your partner invites you to do:

Sunday

Monday

Tuesday

Wednesday

Thursday

Friday

Saturday

4 Groupwork

Group A

Anne is a very attractive young lady. So when she has a puncture on the way to the office one morning there is soon a crowd of men around her (and one woman) offering suggestions.

Here are some suggestions they make:

PETER: I'd be happy to change the wheel for you myself. I had a puncture only last week, so I'm quite an expert at changing wheels.

JOHN: You'll get dirty if you try and change the wheel yourself. If I were you I'd call the garage.

ALAN: I think you should leave the car here. Perhaps I could give you a lift to your office.

CHRISTOPHER: The best thing to do would be to tow the car to a garage. There's a good garage just by my house, and I have a tow rope here.

i) Pretend you are these people, and your partner is Anne. Make the suggestions to Anne using the words you have practised in this unit. Anne must guess each time who you are pretending to be.

ii) Now you are Anne and your partner will give you some suggestions. Decide each time who your partner is pretending to be.

ANDREW offers to drive the car to her office nearby.
DAVID suggests they have a drink together. After that he'll change the wheel.
MARTIN's uncle runs a garage. A mechanic could be sent.
MARY suggests Anne changes the wheel herself. It's a small job.

Group B

Anne is a very attractive young lady. So when she has a puncture on the way to the office one morning there is soon a crowd of men around her (and one woman) offering suggestions.

i) Pretend you are Anne. Your partner will give you some suggestions. Decide each time who your partner is pretending to be.

ALAN suggests they leave the car there. He offers Anne a lift to her office.
PETER offers to change the wheel himself. He says he's quite an expert at it.
CHRISTOPHER suggests he tows the car to a garage near his house.
JOHN thinks Anne should call a garage. Changing a wheel is a dirty business.

ii) Now pretend you are these people, and your partner is Anne. Make the suggestions to Anne using the words you have practised in this unit. Anne must guess each time who you are pretending to be.

MARTIN: My uncle owns a garage. He could send a mechanic to come and fix it. If you like I'll phone him up.

DAVID: I suggest we go and have a cup of coffee together. Then when we're feeling better, I'll change the wheel for you.

MARY: You can easily change the wheel yourself. It won't take more than a minute.

ANDREW: Your office isn't far away. You can easily drive the car that distance on a flat tyre. I'll drive the car for you if you like.

5 i) People always seem to be making invitations and suggestions to Anne. Here are some of the things said to her recently. In what situations do you think they were said?

a) Why not take it back if it's too small.	If I were you I'd ....
b) Let's phone for a taxi. Otherwise I'm afraid you'll miss it.	I suggest we ....
c) Would you like to borrow mine? I don't mind as long as you buy some petrol.	You're quite welcome to ....
d) How about looking in the yellow pages. Maybe you'll find it there.	You could always ....
e) Why not go and have a lie down. I'm sure you'll feel better then.	You'd better ....
f) Let's put it on its side. Maybe it'll go through then.	If I were you ....
g) Would you like to come with me? I can show you exactly where it is.	You're quite welcome ....
h) How about writing a cheque. I'm sure they won't mind.	I suggest ....

ii) Now make these invitations and suggestions in another way, using the words on the right.

Unit 13

Trains and tubes

A Trains

1 Practise these:

How might the ticket-clerk reply?

Practise these replies:

Now practise the questions and replies together.

★ Buying a train ticket is not as simple as you might think. There is a wide range of tickets valid at different times. The most expensive sort of ticket is a single. If you can buy a return ticket, you will almost certainly save money. The cheapest return ticket is a day-return, which means you must return the same day. But there are also weekend returns, 17-day returns, monthly returns and economy returns. The ticket clerk will help you. But remember, get a return if you can.

2   Finding out about trains.

Group A

i)   a)   Ask your partner the times of trains to *five* of these places. Write down what he
tells you.

Manchester ....   Exeter ....
Durham ....   Cardiff ....
Leeds ....   Edinburgh ....
Liverpool ....   Oxford ....
Newcastle ....   Brighton ....

b)   Find out from your partner what time *five* of these trains arrive.

11.45 to Manchester ....   13.40 to Exeter ....
14.00 to Durham ....   21.08 to Cardiff ....
15.25 to Leeds ....   8.36 to Edinburgh ....
17.07 to Liverpool ....   9.47 to Oxford ....
10.27 to Newcastle ....   15.19 to Brighton ....

c)   Find out how much it will cost you to get to *five* of these places.

day return to Manchester ....   single to Exeter ....
single to Durham ....   day return to Cardiff ....
weekend return to Leeds ....   weekend return to Edinburgh ....
single to Liverpool ....   single to Oxford ....
return to Newcastle ....   return to Brighton ....

ii)   Now you give information to your partner. (Look at page 109.)

Group B

i) Give your partner the information he asks for.

   a) They leave at. . .

Edinburgh – 5.35, 7.20, 8.36	Liverpool – 14.20, 16.35, 17.07
Leeds – 15.25, 16.05, 18.15	Newcastle – 9.42, 10.27, 11.08
Oxford – 9.47, 10.10, 11.21	Brighton – 13.06, 15.19, 17.17
Durham – 9.30, 12.15, 14.00	Manchester – 10.30, 11.45, 13.15
Cardiff – 8.17, 14.58, 21.08	Exeter – 10.49, 13.40, 17.08

   b) It's due in at. . .

21.08 to Cardiff – 22.30	15.19 to Brighton – 17.12
17.07 to Liverpool – 19.47	10.27 to Newcastle – 18.19
9.47 to Oxford – 10.08	13.40 to Exeter – 16.12
14.00 to Durham – 19.30	8.36 to Edinburgh – 13.45
11.45 to Manchester – 13.43	15.25 to Leeds – 19.19

   c) It costs. . .

return to Newcastle – £17.36	single to Durham – £8.00
single to Exeter – £3.45	day return to Cardiff – £6.40
day return to Manchester – £7.50	weekend return to Edinburgh – £15.10
return to Brighton – £3.15	single to Liverpool – £7.45
single to Oxford – £2.75	weekend return to Leeds – £9.36

ii) Now you ask for information. (Look at page 108.)

B Tubes

1 Even people who live in London sometimes get lost on the tube! On the tape you will hear some people asking for help at the enquiry office at Oxford Circus station. Listen to the tape and fill in the blanks.

a) From Oxford Circus to Chancery Lane:
Take the .... Line eastbound. It's only .... stops.

b) From Oxford Circus to Lancaster Gate:
Take the .... Line westbound. It's the stop after ....
....

c) From Oxford Circus to High Street, Kensington:
Take the Central Line .... as far as Notting Hill Gate.
Then change on to the .... or Circle Lines southbound.
It's .... stop after Notting Hill Gate.

d) Now find these stations on the map on page 111.

2 How do the people on the tape ask the way?

Excuse me, how do you. . .?
Excuse me, would you tell me. . .?

Now ask your teacher the way to these stations from Oxford Circus, and find them on the map:

South Kensington
Holloway Road
Archway
Tower Hill

3 Look at the map of the London Underground on page 111.
What are the names of the missing stations?

1 =   5 =
2 =   6 =
3 =   7 =
4 =

★ The cost of your journey by bus or tube in London depends on how far you go. Your tube ticket is checked when you go on to the platform *and* when you reach your destination, so don't lose it or throw it away.
   London Transport, who organise tube and bus services in central London, offer a range of cheap tickets which are useful for sight-seeing. You'll find full details at Oxford Circus station enquiry office.

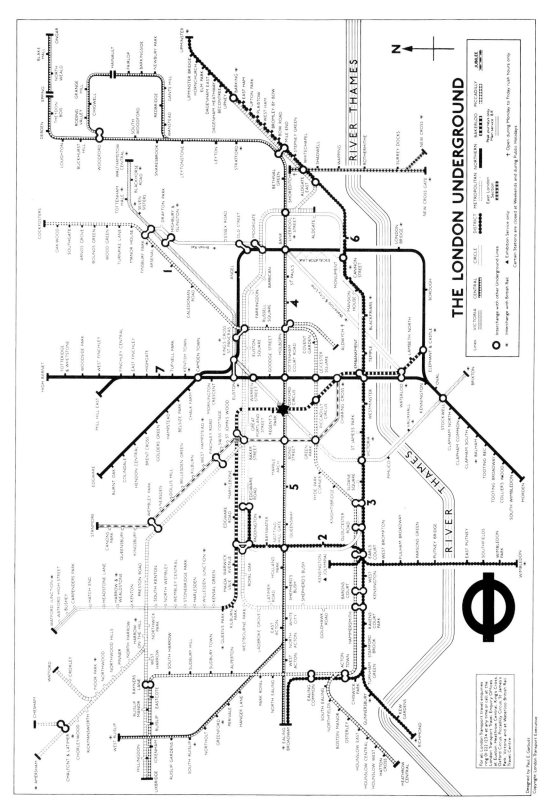

THE LONDON UNDERGROUND

Designed by Paul E Garbutt

Copyright London Transport Executive

Saying yes and no to invitations

 1 i) Listen to the tape. What is happening? Where? When? Do the speakers know each other well? Think about what they might say.

ii) Listen again and write down what they actually say.

Yes, I'd .... What sort of time?

Thanks a lot. That would ....
....

Oh, I'm afraid ....

I'm sorry, I'm ....
....

2 The people you have just heard said yes or no to invitations. Now you practise saying yes or no to invitations. Use these words:

Yes, I'd. . .
Thanks a lot. That. . . nice.
Oh,. . . I can't.
I'm. . ., I'm. . . then.

a) It's Monday night. You've heard *Live and Let Die* is on at the Odeon.
b) A game of tennis on Saturday helps you to relax after a hard week.
c) Your football team is playing on Tuesday. But you only have ten men. You need someone else.
d) John is having a party on Wednesday, but you've no one to go with.
e) You feel like a walk in the country on Sunday.
f) You haven't been to the zoo for a long time. Thursday would be a good day.
g) You usually meet your friends at the pub on Fridays. Why not take someone with you.

3 Here's your diary for next week.

Sunday
Monday
Tuesday
Wednesday
Thursday
Friday
Saturday

Write down what you are doing on *three* days.
Now do exercise 2 again. This time say yes when you're free, no when you're busy.
If you're busy explain why.

4 Groupwork

Group A

i) Decide how you would invite a friend in these situations:

    a) There's a tennis court free on Friday and you haven't played for a long time.

    b) There's a Beethoven concert on at the Town Hall on Monday. The tickets are cheap and you'd love to go.

    c) You've heard there are some good shops in Brighton. You want to go next week, to buy some clothes.

    d) You haven't seen your friend for some time. Perhaps you could have a drink one evening next week in the pub.

    e) You and your friends are playing football on Saturday afternoon. Perhaps your friend would like to join you.

Your partner is a friend. Invite him. How does he reply each time? Write a number:

He declines because he's already going out?
He accepts and asks which day you can go?
He declines because he must look after a sick relative?
He accepts and asks about arrangements to meet?
He declines because he must stay at home?

ii) Now your partner invites you. Reply using the words in brackets.

. . . go to the seaside	– (Yes / who else going?)
. . . come to a party	– (No / too much work. . .)
. . . go to the theatre	– (Yes / . . . Friday?)
. . . go out for a meal	– (No / get up early next day. . .)
. . . play cricket	– (No / friends staying for weekend. . .)

Group B

i) Your partner is a friend, and he invites you to do these things with him. Reply
   using the words in brackets.

   . . . go shopping   – (Yes / what day. . .?)
   . . . play tennis   – (No / mother ill. . . Look after her)
   . . . go for a drink   – (Yes / where meet. . . when?)
   . . . play football   – (No / must stay home. . .)
   . . . go to a concert   – (No / already going out. . .)

ii) Now decide how you would invite a friend in these situations:
   a) There's a good play on at the theatre next week, and there are plenty of tickets
      left for each night.
   b) Some friends have arranged a game of cricket for next Saturday. But you need
      one more person to make up the team.
   c) The weather's fine, and you're on holiday next week. You're going with a
      group of friends to the sea.
   d) You love Chinese food. Perhaps your friend will join you in a meal at a
      Chinese restaurant on Monday.
   e) Peter's having a house-warming party on Tuesday. He said you could bring
      along friends.

   Your partner is a friend. Invite him. How does he reply each time? Write a
   number:

   He accepts and suggests a day?
   He declines because he has too much to do?
   He accepts and asks who else is going?
   He declines because he has to get up early the next day?
   He declines because he has guests?

5   You invite your friend to the cinema on Friday. Is he going to say yes or no? He
   begins his answer like this:

   I've got rather a headache, and. . .
   I'd love to, but. . .
   I've got rather a headache, but. . .
   Fine, what time. . .?
   Shall I meet you outside the cinema, or. . .?
   Oh, I'm afraid. . .
   That sounds great. Which cinema. . .?
   Friday? Oh dear, I think my mother-in-law. . .
   Friday? Well, I'm certainly free, and. . .
   Thanks, but I really ought to. . .

   How do you think he continues? Finish the sentences.

Unit 14

Cars

A Hiring a car

1 Practise these:

How might the receptionist reply?

Practise these replies:

Now practise the questions and replies together.

★ To hire a car, of course, you need a driving licence. In some cases your national driving licence may be acceptable, but if you know you are going to hire a car in Britain, the best thing to do is to get an International Driving Licence before you leave home.

You can hire cars all over Britain. There are big national (and international) firms, and also small local firms. You can arrange to have a car waiting for you at airports and most big railway stations.

Don't forget we drive on the left!

116

Group A

i) a) You want to hire a car. Ask your partner if there are cars available at *five* of these times.

next Tuesday   over the weekend
tomorrow   next Monday
on Friday   on Wednesday
today   the day after tomorrow
on Tuesday   on Saturday

   b) Now say how long you want to hire the car for. Choose *five* periods. Say that you want to hire a car for *five* of these periods.

one day   a day and a half
a week   three days
the weekend   a fortnight
four days   five days
two days   three weeks

   c) Ask how much it will cost to hire these cars. Write down the information.

Mini
Cortina
Rover 3500
Allegro
Escort

   d) Now practise complete conversations.

ii) Now your partner wants to hire a car (look at the next page).

Group B

i) a) Your partner wants to hire a car on five different days. Tell him that he can. Write down when he wants to hire it.

    b) Ask your partner how long he wants to hire a car for. Write down what he says.

    c) Tell your partner how much it costs to hire these cars.
        Escort   – £15.25 per day and 5p per mile.
        Allegro   – £50 per week and 4p per mile.
        Rover 3500   – £18.50 per day and 7p per mile.
        Cortina   – £46 per week. Unlimited mileage.
        Mini   – £11.75 per day. Unlimited mileage.

    d) Now practise complete conversations.

ii) Now you want to hire a car (look at the previous page).

3 On the tape you will hear someone hiring a car. Fill in the blanks.

i) I'd like to .... a car for a few days.
    What sort have you got ....?
    I don't .... anything big.

ii) There's a £50 ....
    Does that include ....?
    No, I'm afraid .... insurance costs £2 per day extra.

iii) I'd rather not pay a ....
    Then you have .... mileage.
    So I'll save money with the ...., won't I?

B Travelling by car

1 i) Look at the map on the next page. You are in Winton. Ask your teacher the way to these places:

| Excuse me | Could you tell me how to get to How do I get to | Parkhurst Hamford Buckham Chome Compton | please? |

Write the names of the places on the map.

ii) ⌒‾ HAMFORD IS SOUTH OF BUCKHAM. ‾⌒

Now describe the position of these places:

Parkhurst / Hamford
Chome   / Parkhurst
Winton   / Langdon
Buckham / Parkhurst
Hamford / Chome

iii) Now describe to your partner where the towns are.

| It's | north east south east east south west north west | of Winton. |

Which towns is your partner describing?

★ British roads are generally very good. Motorways are free. Road signs generally follow international conventions. Detailed guidance about traffic rules and conventions can be found in a booklet called *The Highway Code* available from bookshops in Britain.

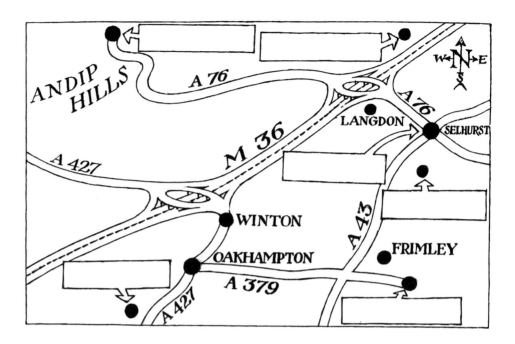

2 Here is what your teacher said in exercise 1(i). Complete the passages.

Here are some words to help you:

goes	left
from	as far as
straight to	right
north	go

a) Winton to Parkhurst
Take the .... south from Winton. It goes .... Parkhurst. It's about 20 miles.

b) Winton to Hamford
Take the A427 south as far as .... Turn .... on to the A379. It's about 30 miles.

c) Winton to Buckham
Go .... on the M36. It .... straight to Buckham. It's about 25 miles.

d) Winton to Chome
Take the M36 north .... Langdon. Turn left on to the .... It's about 25 miles from Langdon.

e) Winton to Compton
Go north on the M36 as far as .... Turn .... on to the A76. .... as far as Selhurst. Turn right on to the A43. Compton's just over 5 miles .... Selhurst.

Making arrangements

1 i) Listen to the tape. What is happening? Where? When? Do the speakers know each other well? Think about what they might say.

ii) Listen again and write down what they actually say.

Let me see. Let's ....

.... in

Queen's Road at about 7.00.

Shall we .... in
front of the library?

Good. So ....
then.

No, I'll .... at about
7.00

2   The people you have heard were arranging to meet. What did they say? Finish their sentences.

i)   A: O.K. What sort of .... ?
     B: Shall we make it 5.00 in front of the library?
     A: 5.00 in front of the library. ....

Practise arranging when to meet:

ii) A: .... shall we meet?
     B: Let me see. Let's say by the traffic lights in Queen's Road at about 7.00.
     A: .... by the traffic lights at about 7.00.

Practise arranging where to meet:

at		the station
outside	the bridge	the church
in	the Town Hall	the bookshop
under	the lake	the bus stop
by	the travel agents	Woolworths
		the buffet

iii) A: Let's go by bus, ... ?
     B: No, I'll pick you up at about 7.00.
     A: O.K. That's very .... you.

Practise arranging how to get there.

3 Look at the map of Hamford below. Choose five members of your class. Write
   down numbers 1–5 and write a name beside each number.
      Arrange to meet these five people at different places and different times. Write a
   number on the map by the place you will meet each person. Write the time beside
   their name.

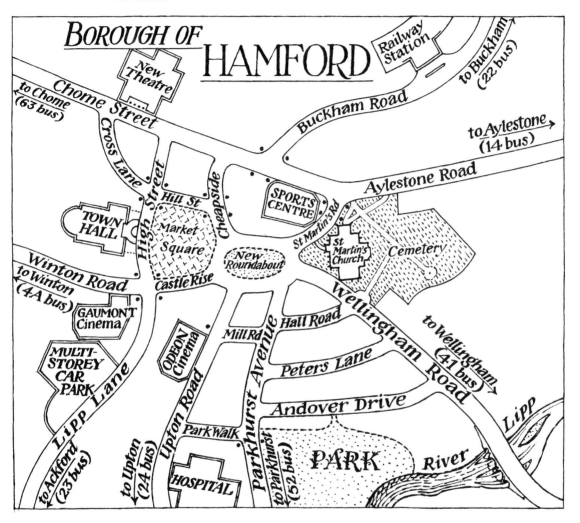

Unit 15 Consolidation

A Interview

Mr Rubber is the Public Relations Officer for the London Division of the Western Region of British Rail. We talked to Mr Rubber about his work, and we have taken three sections from the interview. Listen to each and answer the questions.

Section 1

1 Mr Rubber talks about two main areas of his work here. What are they?
2 Now listen in more detail to the second of these areas. What does Mr Rubber say about:
rhyme
keeping the temperature down
the results for the staff of being rude?
3 Mr Rubber mentions the 'inner workings' of the railway. What is the point he is making here?
4 There is an important difference between being a customer in a supermarket and a customer on the railway. What is it?
5 What do you think is Mr Rubber's attitude towards people who complain to him? Do you think that nationalised industries pay enough attention to complaints?

Section 2

Groupwork

In this section Mr Rubber talks about the special situation the railways find themselves in.

1 Why is their situation special?
2 Are all railways in all countries in the same position? What differences does Mr Rubber suggest?
3 The Slough–Windsor branch is given as an example. What of? What happens to lines like this?
Do you agree with this policy?

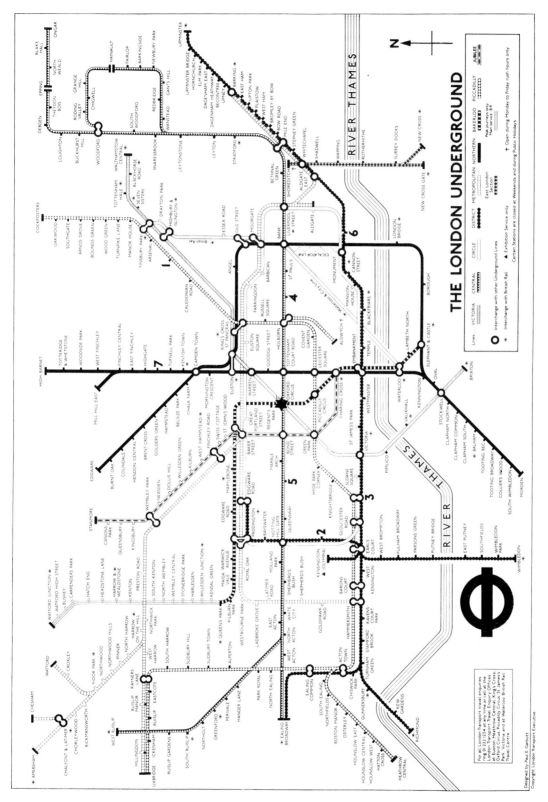

Section 3

1 In this section there are two main topics of conversation. What are they?

2 Listening to the tape, do you think that

	Yes	No	Don't know
a) High Speed Trains have enabled British Rail to make an overall profit?			
b) High Speed Trains are reserved for businessmen?			
c) In order to travel on certain trains it is necessary to pay a supplement?			
d) The speakers feel that reducing fares would help British Rail to make more money?			
e) The supplement on the 'Golden Hind' was imposed because it was a deluxe train?			

B Role-play

After travelling on a British Rail train you want to complain about the service you received.

Decide what your complaint is and what action you want British Rail to take.

Your partner will pretend to be doing Mr Rubber's job. Telephone him and complain.

C Grammar to practise

Verb constructions

1 i)

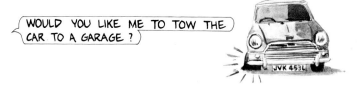

WOULD YOU LIKE ME TO TOW THE CAR TO A GARAGE ?

JVK 453L

Finish these sentences:

It's cold in here. Would you like me to .... ?
You won't arrive in time. Would you like me to .... ?
It's rather dark. Would you like me to .... ?
That case looks really heavy. Would you like me to .... ?
I'm going to the post office. Would you like me to .... ?

ii) ┌─ I'D LIKE JOHN TO COME TO THE PARTY. ─┐
    └─ YES, I'D LIKE HIM TO COME AS WELL. ─┘

Make some more sentences like these:

Peter's got long hair. He should get it cut.
Mary has never met your brother. She should meet him.
Peter and Mike are going out now. They should stay and do the washing up.
My boyfriend's car is old. He should buy a new one.
Janet's leaving school soon. She should go to university.

iii) ┌─ JOHN DOESN'T WANT TO COME TO THE PARTY. ─┐
     └─ BUT I WANT HIM TO COME. ─┘

Make similar responses to these:

Peter doesn't want to get his hair cut.
Mary doesn't want to meet your brother.
Peter and Mike don't want to stay and do the washing up.
My boyfriend doesn't want to buy a new car.
Janet doesn't want to go to university.

► 'Would like' is more polite, but less strong than 'want'. Notice that both, 'would like', and 'want' can be followed directly by the infinitive with 'to' – 'John doesn't want to come', or by a noun/pronoun – 'I want him to come'.

2

Ask questions and give answers:

The plane from Belgrade is due to arrive at 12.20.
According to the programme, the concert doesn't start until 8.00.
The journey home normally doesn't take very long.
The advertisement said the film ends at 10.00.
Your car doesn't normally need any oil.
You think you have enough food at home for your guests.
There's normally enough snow to go skiing at Christmas.
You think John will be back on Sunday.

► One use of 'should' is to talk about something you think will happen, or that normally happens.

3

Make suggestions using these sentences:

phone her up
don't tell the police
open the window
don't worry about it
buy a new car
don't go
take the exam again
don't get upset

▶ Notice the negative forms:

would – wouldn't
should – shouldn't
In this exercise 'should' is used to make suggestions.

4 〈 I'D RATHER NOT PAY A MILEAGE CHARGE . 〉

Use this structure to ask and answer questions, like this:

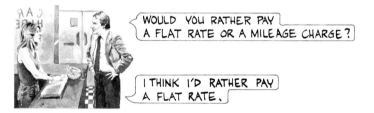

fly to Paris / take the train
travel on Friday / Saturday
have dinner at 7.30 / 9.00
stay in / go to the theatre
have red wine / white wine
do this exercise again / go for a drink

Ask the questions again. This time, say what you'd rather not do.

▶ Notice that the negative of 'would rather' is 'would rather not'. We do not say 'wouldn't rather'.

5

HOW ABOUT GOING FOR A WALK BY THE RIVER?

I DON'T FEEL LIKE GOING FOR A DRINK.

Make sentences using these structures:

cook dinner
go to the theatre
eat out
watch TV
invite Dave and Lynne round
listen to the radio
play some records

▶ Notice that in both these expressions the verb ends in -ing.

6

ISN'T IT POSSIBLE TO PAY A FLAT RATE?

Make more questions using negative verbs:

I feel sure we could invite someone else.
I feel sure he could come before then.
I feel sure it's possible to go somewhere else.
I feel sure we can find another solution.
I feel sure he'll write you a letter.
I feel sure they'll catch the Friday plane.
I feel sure she'll find her own way.

▶ We use this construction with a negative verb in questions when we are expecting to receive the answer 'yes'. You have seen some examples of this construction in unit 4. Try to find them.

7   JOHN: We'll have to pick you up at about 7 o'clock.
      MARTIN: Will you pick up John's friend at 7 o'clock?
      PAUL: Yes, I'll pick him up.

Make sentences like Martin's and Paul's:

turn on light / can't see what / doing
turn up radio / can't hear properly
turn down record player / much too loud
pick up children / on way home / work
look up John's number / directory
take back glasses / borrowed from Angela
take round dishes / promised / lend Mary
phone up Andrew / Sunday

▶   In these sentences the words 'on', 'up', 'down', 'back', 'round' are called *particles*. Notice their position in the sentence. If the object of the sentence is a pronoun, the particle must come after it. If the object is a noun, like 'light', 'radio' or 'record player', then there are two possibilities. The particle can come after the noun, or before it. We can say 'turn the light on', or 'turn on the light'. If the object is very long, then we usually put the particle before it. We would prefer to say 'turn on the light by John's bed', and not 'turn the light by John's bed on'.

There are some other verb constructions with particles, where you can *never* put the particle after the object, whether it is a noun or a pronoun. For example, with the verb 'come across' you can say:
    I came across an old book in my father's room
    I came across it in my father's room.

But not:
    I came an old book across. . .
    I came it across. . .

Each time you learn a verb with a particle you have to find out whether it is like the ones you have practised, or like 'come across'.

1   Indirect speech constructions

COULD YOU TELL ME IF THE OXFORD TRAIN IS LATE, PLEASE?

Ask these questions in the same way:

Is this the Manchester train?
Has the plane from Milan arrived?
Does the 9.30 from Swansea stop at Cardiff?
Will he be able to see me on Thursday?
Will they be back by Saturday?
Is food available on the flight?
Is this the right road for Swindon?
Have you seen a small brown and white dog?

▶   Remember that 'could you. . .' is the polite way to ask a stranger a question. Instead of 'if' you can always use 'whether' – 'Could you tell me whether the Oxford train is late, please?'

2   SHE ASKED ME IF THE OXFORD TRAIN WAS LATE.

Ask the questions in exercise 1 again. Tell your partner what you have been asked.

▶   Notice that because 'asked' is the simple past tense, the main verb 'was' is in the simple past tense also.

Some other constructions

Make more sentences like these:

by rail / on the 9.30 coach
by sea / on the same plane as Alan
by bicycle / on the early morning bus
by train / in Pauline's car
by air / on the Vienna Express

▶ We usually use 'by' to describe a means of transport. But if we want to qualify the means of transport, we use 'on' or 'in':

by plane / on the 10.00 plane
by sea / on the same plane as Alan
by bicycle / on the early morning bus
by train / on the Vienna Express
by car / in my car

Instead of 'by plane' we can say 'by air'. 'By sea' can be used for 'by boat', 'by rail' for 'by train' and 'by road' for 'by car'.

We also often use the verbs 'drive', 'fly', 'sail', 'walk', 'ride' to describe means of transport. E.g. 'he drove / flew there'.

D Grammar to study

How often. . .?   How many times. . .?

These tables are here to help you practise some important points of English grammar. Look at the tables and make sentences from them. Look at the notes with each table and make sure you understand them. Ask your teacher if you need help.

Then look through the units you have studied. Can you use some of the sentences from the tables in these units?

You can do this in class or at home.

I go to London I have been to London I went to London I used to go to London I'll go to London	always / nearly always as often as possible very often / frequently quite often / frequently often / frequently occasionally / from time to time / now and then rarely / seldom hardly / scarcely ever never[1]
Do you go to London I don't go to London	very often / much [2]
I go to London I went to London I used to go to London I'll go to London	every day / week / fortnight / month / year every other day once / twice / three times (a day / a week, etc.) daily / weekly / monthly / annually[3]
I have been to London	once / twice / three times (today / this week, etc.)[4]

The Guardian is published every day except Sundays. It's a daily paper.
The Observer is published every week. It's a weekly paper.
Punch is published every month. It's a monthly magazine.
I'm going to take my annual holidays next month.

Notes

1 Note the position of these adverbs in a sentence:

a) If they are single words, they normally occur in mid-position, e.g.
    I *always* go. . .
    I have *often* been. . .
    I *sometimes* went. . .
    I *never* used to. . .

    Hardly ever and *scarcely ever* also normally occur in mid-position, e.g. I *hardly ever* go to London.

b) Adverbs of more than one word normally occur in end-position, e.g. I go to London *as often as possible*.

2 (very) *much*	This is used only with questions or negatives.
3 *every day*, etc.	These are all statements of definite frequency. Contrast these with the expressions in (1) which are all statements of indefinite frequency.
4 *once/twice today*, etc.	Notice the use of the present perfect tense here. You are talking about frequency within a period of time which is still continuing.

Tapescripts

Unit 3   Arriving in Britain

A: Excuse me.

B: Yes, can I help you?

A: Yes. Could you tell me where the bar is, please?

B: The bar. Yes, you see the stairs over there? Well the bar is just on the right, at the foot of the stairs.

A: Thank you.

B: Can I help you?

C: Yes, I want to catch the London bus. Could you tell me where the bus-stop is, please?

B: Yes, it's just outside, next to the main car park.

C: I see. Thank you very much.

B: You're welcome. Can I help you?

D: Could you tell me where the bookstall is, please?

B: Yes, it's just over there on the right, next to the bar.

D: Thank you.

E: Excuse me, could you tell my wife where the Ladies is, please?

B: Yes of course. Just go over there to the main exit and you'll see the Ladies on the right, by the main door.

E: Thank you very much.

F: Excuse me, could you tell me where to catch the bus for Reading, please?

B: Yes, just outside the main exit, on the left.

F: Thank you.

G: Could you tell me when the next bus for London leaves, please?

B: Yes, they leave every fifteen minutes. I think there's one leaving in about five minutes.

G: Fine, thank you very much.

H: I'm looking for the bank. Could you tell me where it is, please?

B: Yes, it's over there in the corner, next to the British Rail desk.

H: Thank you.

I: Excuse me, could you tell me when the next bus for Reading leaves, please?

B: Yes, certainly, let me see. On the hour and the half hour, so, what time is it now, yes, umm about fifteen minutes, sir.

I: Fine, thank you very much.

B: I think I deserve some coffee after all that.

Unit 3 Saying hello

(The words in italic are missing on the first version of the tape.)

i) A: Hello, Mr Aitken.
    B: Hello, Mike. Did you *have a good journey*?
    A: Not bad thanks. The flight was a bit bumpy, but at least we arrived on time.
    B: And how are your parents?
    A: Oh, fine. They both send their regards. . .

ii) A: Good evening, Mr Davis. I'm glad you could come. It's nice to see you again.
     B: Hello, Mr Samuels. Nice to see you too. Have many people arrived yet?
     A: No, you're the first, actually. Anyway, come in and *have a drink*.
     B: Thanks, I will. That's just what I need. I'll have a scotch, if I may. . .

iii) A: Ah, Mary. Come and join us.
      B: Oh, hello Andy. Yes, I'd love to.
      A: I haven't seen Colin for a long time. How *is he*?
      B: Oh, he's fine, thanks. Cheers. Merry Christmas.
      A: Thanks, and the same to you. Drink up, and I'll buy you another one. . .

iv) A: Good heavens. . . Peter! I haven't seen you for ages.
     B: No, I've been away for the past two months. Good to see you again, Alan. How *are you keeping*?
     A: Very well, thanks. And you're certainly looking brown and healthy. Where have you been? Majorca?
     B: No such luck! Only Birmingham, I'm afraid. . .

Unit 4 Personal information

Sally: John, the phone's ringing. Can you get it?

John: O.K., will do. Hello, Winton 86403.

Peter: Oh, hello John. Peter Roberts here. I've just had a phone call from a chap who wants to join the club, and I've got the details here. Can you make a note of them.

John: Yes, O.K. Just wait a second while I get a pencil. Right.

Peter: O.K. – his first names are Abdulla Mohammed and his surname is Hamedi, that's H-A-M-E-D-I.

John: He must be an Arab then.

Peter: That's right, he's Iraqi actually – a businessman spending a year over here. He's brought his wife and children with him and they're staying at 46 Maynard Close, Buckham. I told him you'd get in touch with details of the subscription and so on. He's on the phone and his number is Buckham 50491.

John: Right.

Here's another person who would like to join the sports club.

Robert: Hello, is that the secretary of the Winton sports club?. . . I'd like to apply for membership of the club, please. . . It's Roberto Alfonso Pasquale. The surname's Pasquale. . . P-A-S-Q-U-A-L-E. . . Yes, it's 24a Portland Park, Chome. Telephone Chome 7652. . . I'm Venezuelan. . . an accountant. . . single. . . Not at all, it's 29 June 1940. . . Right, thank you very much indeed. Goodbye.

Unit 4   Introducing yourself and others

i) A: Angela, come and sit with us. We were just deciding what to do about the party next weekend. Oh, I don't think you two have met yet. Angela, this is Susan. She's a student at Birmingham.
    B: Hello, Susan. What *are you studying there?*
    C: English Literature. I've been there for a couple of years. . .

ii) A: Hello again, Andrew. How was the crossing?
    B: Quite good, thanks. At least I wasn't seasick.
    A: Well, welcome back to England. By the way I don't think you've met my wife, Jenny.
    C: No, we haven't met. Hello Andrew. How do you do?
    B: How *do you do.* It's very nice of you both to come and meet me like this. . .

iii) A: John, come over here a minute. There's someone I'd like you to meet.
     B: Yes, all right.
     A: Marion, this is the person I was telling you about earlier, John MacDonald.
     C: Hello, John, I'm *pleased to meet you.* Alan's told me all about you already. . .

iv) A: There you are at last David. We thought you were never coming.
    B: Sorry, I got held up at work.
    A: Anyway, I'd like to *introduce my fiancée, Margaret.*
    B: Hello, Margaret. Fiancée, eh? Well, this is a surprise. Congratulations. . .

Unit 5   People

i) He is 37 years old, approximately 5' 8" tall with short black hair. He is well-built and extremely strong. This man is dangerous and may attack without warning. He should not be approached by members of the public.

ii) Oh she's a dreadful person. She's got lots of money, but she's really mean. She hates spending money. She's not very tall – about 5' and she's rather thin. I suppose she's got blond hair, but she's not at all attractive. That face! Oh, god! She's awful.

iii) She'll be at the station at 5.30. She's got long red hair and she's very good-looking. She's fairly tall – about 5' 8" and very slim. Yes, I'm sure you'll enjoy meeting her.

iv) What else can I say? He doesn't always agree with what I say, but he always listens to my opinions. He's really good-looking too – very tall, about 6′ 2″. He's slim and he's got lovely fair hair. Just the man for me.

v) In appearance he was an imposing figure. About 6′ tall with long fair hair, he left a lasting impression on everyone he met – especially women, who generally found him very good-looking. He was particularly known for his warm, friendly character. Whenever a friend was in trouble, he never failed to help.

Unit 5   Saying goodbye

i) A: Oh, James. That was a great party, but *I'm afraid I must go now.*
   B: Come on, you don't have to go already, do you?
   A: Sorry, but I really must be off. I must be at work early tomorrow.
   B: O.K. Well, goodbye then, Paul. Thanks for coming. . .

ii) A: Would you like another drink before you go, Bob? One for the road.
    B: No thanks. I really must go now. . . Well, thank you for *a very pleasant evening*, Mr Wilkinson.
    A: Thank *you* for coming. Goodbye for now.
    B: Goodbye, and thanks again.

iii) A: Good heavens. Is that the time, Frank? I really must fly, otherwise I'm going to be late.
     B: O.K. then. I'll see you next week, won't I?
     A: Yes, *I hope so*. See you, Frank.
     B: Yes, see you. . .
     A: 'Bye.

iv) A: Well, I hope you've enjoyed your stay.
    B: I certainly have. And thanks again for everything.
    A: Don't forget to look us up next time you're in London.
    B: O.K. Thanks. All the very best, then.
    A: Thanks, and the *same to you*. 'Bye. . .

Unit 6   Interview

Section 1

JR: You work in the Registrar's office, don't you?
TB: Yes. I'm. . . I've been here ten years as a Senior Assistant Registrar.
JP: Really. What does that involve? What do you have to do?
TP: Well my particular job is acting as secretary to the four Faculty Boards and I deal with all the admissions of postgraduate students in the University.
JR: Particularly postgraduate?
TB: Entirely postgraduate. I've nothing at all to do with undergraduates.
JR: Do you find that you get a particular, er, sort of. . . different national groups? I

mean, do you get larger numbers from Latin America or. . .?

TB: Yes, well. Er, of our intake last year, nearly half were from overseas. Big contingents from African countries, and from the Far East, and from the Middle East, and from Latin America.

JR: Umm. But you've been doing. . . have you been doing just that for the last. . . for ten years or have you changed in your role?

TB: Oh, no. Before. . . Since I've been at Reading, yes, I've been doing the same job. Er, before that I was secretary of the Medical School at Birmingham, and before that I worked in Local Government. . .

JR: Oh, I see.

TB: So I've done different types of things.

JR: Yes indeed. How do you think you. . . how do you imagine your job would develop in the future? Do you. . . can you imagine shifting into a different kind of responsibility, or doing something. . .?

TB: Well I am going to do from October, because I've just come back from a $3\frac{1}{2}$-week visit to Nigeria. And when I came back I found I'd been promoted to Deputy Registrar.

JR: Obviously one has to go to Nigeria more often!

TB: That's right. From 1 October. . . so from then I shall be doing an entirely different kind of job. I shall be secretary of Senate and Council.

JR: What does that involve?

TB: That's going to be more committee work. More policy work, and less dealing with students, unfortunately. I shall miss my contact with students.

JR: So it will be more the administration of the University. . .

TB: That's right. More central policy, secretary of Senate, secretary of Council. I shall go to Deans and Standing Committee, deal with academic staff appointments and that sort of thing.

JR: What exactly is the Senate and the Council you talked about?

TB: The Senate is the academic governing body of the University. It's all the professors and the non-professorial staff who've been elected, and it's concerned with the academic government of the University. The Council has on it the Deans, and lay members, people who are not working in the University, members from Local Authorities and business and commerce. They're concerned with the financial management of the University and the property and that aspect of it.

JR: So you have contact with the two halves, so to speak.

TB: Two halves, the outside world and the inside world. That's right.

Section 2

JR: What kind of training does one need to go into this type of job?

TB: That's a very good question. I don't think there is any – specifically.

JR: For example in your case. What was your educational background?

TB: Well, I did a degree in French, at Nottingham, er, and did, after that, eight years, I did careers work in schools, erm, careers guidance officer, like the careers guidance people here at the University, except with secondary schools. Then I went into Local Government because I found I was more interested in the administrative side, then progressed on to universities. So there wasn't any plan and there was no specific training. There are plenty of training courses in management techniques and committee work and so on, which you can attend now. That's developed quite a lot in the last twenty years, and the Committee of Vice-Chancellors runs all sorts of training activities for university administrators.

JR: But in the first place you did a French degree?

TB: But there isn't a degree you can do for it. I think you. . . most of the administrators I've come across have degrees in all sorts of things.

JR: Well it's. . . I know in my case I did an English Literature degree, and I didn't really expect to end up doing what I'm doing now.

TB: Quite.

JR: Were you local to Nottingham actually? Is there any reason why you went to Nottingham University?

TB: No, no I come from the North of England, from what is now West Yorkshire, was then the West Riding of Yorkshire. And, er, Nottingham was one of the universities I put on my list and liked the look of, and I'm very glad I went there. Pleasant spot.

JR: Yes, indeed. Let's see. Were you from the industrial part of Yorkshire?

TB: Yes, from the woollen district.

JR: Where?

TB: Halifax, near Halifax.

JR: Ah, Halifax. That's Hell, Hull and Halifax.

TB: That's right, the three places you don't go to.

Section 3

JR: Are your children still at school? Well, you said the girl was 15, and the boy 17. Are they still at school?

TB: Yes, Martin, my eldest boy, left school last year. He works at, well goes to a Day Centre nearby for physically handicapped adults. My daughter, she does her 'O' levels next year. She's in the fourth year at a comprehensive school.

JR: How's her French?

TB: Very good. She likes French and German. She's not very scientific. Christopher, who's in the last year of junior school, goes to secondary school next year. He's much more practically orientated. Maths and Science are more up his street.

JR: They'll be going to a comprehensive, I suppose.

TB: We have the choice of three comprehensives.

JR: Really! It's unusual to have so many to choose from.

TB: Well, yes. Alison seems to have done all right. We, er. . . there are certain criticisms one has, but, er, on the whole we're not too dissatisfied.

JR: Well, not naming any names. but what do you think one considers when one is trying to choose. Well I don't know if one can really choose one's school, actually. You tend to. . . the kid goes where it's sent.

TB: You can't, er, very easily, unless you're very rich and can afford to choose a private school. And since we're not very rich – we've got all three children to consider – we can't do that. So they go to the local comprehensive school. One is in the hands of, you know, quality of staff, the size of the school. I think the size of the school has a lot to do with it.

JR: How big are these. . .?

TB: This one is about 1200 children, which is in my view rather too big.

JR: Well I remember I. . . probably you went to a grammar school as well.

TB: That's right. Probably about three or four hundred. But everybody knows everybody and the thing gels more as a family.

JR: Indeed. Indeed, yes. I suspect it was a mistake to. . . 1200 is about the number, but some of these schools are 2000. I really suspect that it's just too large for the children – and for the staff.

TB: That's right. There's no sense of community. But, we'll just have to see.

Unit 7 Doctors

i)   Doctor: Just take your shirt off, will you. I want to listen to your chest. [Pause] Thank you. You can put it on again now.

ii) Doctor: Now I want to take your temperature. Put this thermometer under your tongue, please.

iii) Doctor: I'm going to give you an injection. Could roll up your sleeve, please.

iv) Doctor: Take this prescription to the chemist. He will give you some tablets and some medicine. I want you to take 3 tablets three times a day and take a teaspoonful of the medicine just before you go to bed.

v)   Doctor: Go home and go straight to bed. Keep warm and take things easy for a few days. If you don't feel better after the weekend, come back and see me again.

Unit 7 Finding out

i)   Announcer: Mind the doors, please.
     A: Look, there's a tube map over there. Let's go and have a look.
     B: O.K. [To other passengers] Excuse me, sorry. . . Right, here we are. Paddington. Now, there's Oxford Circus. Look, the Bakerloo Line goes right there.
     A: Yes, right. So we want a Bakerloo Line train. What's that one?
     B: I don't know. [To passenger] Excuse me, could you tell me if that's *a Bakerloo Line train*, please?
     C: I've no idea, I'm afraid. Look at that board over there.
     B: Thanks. Come on, Jack.

ii) A: Morning.
     B: Good morning. Umm. . . three-quarters of a pound of mince, please.
     A: Three-quarters of a pound of mince? Right. Lovely day.
     B: Yes, not bad. Still a bit cold though.
     A: There we are. Anything else?

B: I don't know. Those pork chops look quite nice. How *much are they*, please?

A: 95p a pound.

B: 95p! No, I think I'd better leave it, thanks. . .

iii) A: Well, at least this is the right terminal. Are you sure you haven't got the details?

B: I've looked everywhere. I thought I put the piece of paper you gave me in my handbag, but. . .

A: Oh, you are useless. You manage to lose absolutely everything. You wait here. [Goes over to the enquiry desk] Excuse me, I wonder *if you could tell me* what time the flight from Rome is due, please?

C: Yes. 16.30.

A: Thank you. [goes back] Come on, let's go and have some coffee. We've got hours to wait.

iv) A: It must be along here somewhere. Just down Princess Road he said, and then on the left. Well, that was Princess road, wasn't it? Can you see it on the map?

B: You know I'm hopeless with maps, dear. Anyway, I haven't got my glasses.

A: Hmph. Look, there's a policeman over there. I'll ask him. Excuse me, I'm looking for Queen Victoria Street. Do you know *where it is,* please?

C: Yes, sir. Go down here and it's the third on the left.

A: Thank you very much. . .

Unit 8   Telephones

i) A: What's Pete's number? I want to give him a ring about Saturday.

B: Isn't it there on the card next to the phone?

A: Oh yes, 832-7642.

C: Hello, 832-7462.

A: 74. . . Oh, I'm sorry. I've got the wrong number. I'm terribly sorry.

C: That's all right.

A: I got the wrong number. I must be getting old. Let's try again.

D: Atkins Ltd. Good afternoon. Can I help you?

A: Could I speak to Mr Thompson, please? Extension 8692 I think.

B: I'm putting you through.

E: Hello, 8692.

A: Could I speak to Peter Thompson, please?

E: I'm sorry. He's not here at the moment. Can I take a message?

A: Yes, please. Could you tell him that Tony phoned and ask him to call me back. He knows the number.

E: Yes, O.K. I'll do that.

A: Thanks very much. Goodbye now.

E: Goodbye.

ii) A: This is bloody stupid. That's the fourth time I've tried. There must be something wrong with the line.

B: Why don't you try through the operator then? She'll be able to help you.

A: Yes O.K. 1-0-0

C: Number, please.

A: Could I have Grantham 3422.

C: Grantham 3422. You can dial that yourself you know, if you use the STD code.

A: Yes, I've tried several times but I can't get through.

C: Right. What is your exchange and number, please?

A: Eastwood 4382.

C: Eastwood 4382. Could you have 16p ready, please. I'm sorry, caller. The line's engaged.

A: O.K., cancel the call, please. I'll try again later.

C: Thank you. Goodbye.

iii) A: Can you remember John and Sally's number?

B: No, it's 43 something – but I don't know after that. You'll have to ring Directory Enquiries.

A: Yes, I suppose so. 192 isn't it?

B: Yes that's right.

C: Directory Enquiries. For which town, please?

A: It's for Ipswich.

C: What is the name and initials, please?

A: It's Whittaker, J. A. Whittaker.

C: And the address, please?

A: 32 Hall Lane, Ipswich.

C: Here is the number. It's Ipswich 43892.

A: 43892. Thank you very much. Goodbye.

C: Goodbye.

Unit 8 Asking people to do things

i) A: Are you sure it'll be all right?

B: Yes, of course. There's no problem. It's only a case of changing the date on the ticket.

A: But what if the plane is already full?

B: Oh, don't worry. Look, you wait here with the luggage. I'll go over to the ticket desk.

C: Good morning, sir. Can I help you?

B: Yes. Could you *change the date on this ticket* for me, please? I've booked to fly tomorrow, but I'd like to go today if possible.

C: Just one moment, sir. I'll check whether there's a seat available on today's flight. . .

ii) A: Are you ready?

B: I won't be a minute. I've just got to change my shoes.

A: Well, I'm going to phone for a taxi, so don't be too long.

B: All right, all right. No need to panic.

C: Hello, Reception. Can I help you?

A: This is Steiner, Room 149. Could I possibly *have a taxi, please*? We want to go to the National Theatre.

C: Certainly, Mr Steiner. When did you want to go?

A: In about five minutes, please – no, you'd better make that ten. My wife still isn't ready.

C: Ten minutes. Thank you, Mr Steiner.

A: Thank you. Goodbye.

iii) A: Here we are. Here's an empty compartment. Pass me that case. It'll go on the luggage rack here. And that one too, will you? That'll go on this side. Are you all right? What's the matter?

B: Oh, it's nothing. It's just the air in here. It's supposed to be a non-smoking compartment. Someone has been smoking in here.

A: Yes, it is a bit stuffy.

B: Stuffy. That's not the word. Look, *open the window*, will you, dear? Let's get some air in here.

A: O.K. I'll see what I can do.

iv) A: Hello. 47653.

B: Hello. Ian? It's Gordon here. Gordon Clifford from next door.

A: Oh yes. Hello.

B: Look, Ian. I've got a bit of a problem. Could you possibly do me a favour? I've got to catch a train in half an hour, and I've just found the car won't start. You couldn't *give me a lift to the station*, could you?

A: Well, actually, that's a bit difficult. I'm afraid my wife's got the car.

B: Oh well, never mind. Thanks anyway. Goodbye.

A: 'Bye.

Unit 9 Garages

A: Hello, Ace Service Station.

B: Hello. Could you possibly help me. I've run out of petrol. You couldn't send some out to me, could you?

A: Yes, I should think so. Where are you?

B: Just outside Chome, on the road to Winton. Just past the junction with the Hamford road.

A: O.K. What sort of car is it?

B: It's a Morris 1100 – a blue one. Registration number KFN 396M

A: Right. How much petrol do you want?

B: Well, could you possibly bring *five gallons* with you. I'll put the bonnet up so that you'll see me.

A: Right, I'll be with you in about ten minutes.

Unit 9   Asking for permission

i) A: Oh, hello Ken. How are you?
    B: Hello, Jim. I'm fine, thanks. Look, it's. . .
    C: Who is it, dear?
    A: It's Ken Roberts from next door. Come in, Ken.
    B: Thanks. Look, I don't want to disturb you. It's just that I'm mending the fence in the back garden. You know, it blew down in the wind last week, and it's a bit difficult to get at it from my garden. I wondered, well, could I possibly *come round into your garden*. It's such a nuisance trying to mend it when I can't reach it properly.
    A: Yes, of course you can. Come round any time. . .

ii) A: They're here. You let them in while I go and turn the oven on.
    B: Yes, O.K. Hello, Jane. Hello, Pete. How are you? Come on in.
    C: Hello, Chris. Thanks. God, it's cold out there. Here you are. We've brought some flowers for Sue.
    B: Thanks very much. That really is nice of you. She's in the kitchen, actually, seeing to the food. Look, let me take your coats.
    D: Thanks, Chris. Actually, do you mind if I *use your phone*? I promised to tell the babysitter where we are and I forgot to give her your number.
    B: Sure, go ahead. You know where it is, don't you?
    D: Yes, thanks. . .

iii) A: That really was beautiful. I haven't tasted fish like that for a long time. You certainly know how to cook, Sue.
    B: Well, I'm glad you enjoyed it. I haven't tried that recipe before, actually.
    A: Well, it certainly was a successful experiment.
    C: Now don't flatter her too much, she'll get big-headed.
    A: Anyway, I enjoyed that. . . You don't mind if I *smoke, do you*?
    C: No, go ahead. In fact, here, have one of mine. . .

iv) A: Are you all right, Anne? You look terribly hot.
    B: I am terribly hot. It's like an oven in here, even with the window open. Can't you do something?
    A: Like what?
    B: Well, I don't suppose people'd mind if you opened the door.
    A: O.K. I'd like to *open the door*. Does anybody mind?
    C: Mind? I don't mind.
    D: Nor do I. Go ahead.
    A: Right, well. Well, that's a bit better. . .

Unit 10   Shops

A: Can I help you?
B: Yes, I'm looking for a blouse. Have you got this one in any other colours?
A: Yes, I think so. What size did you want?

B: I think I need a size 12.

A: Here you are look. This is the same as the one you were looking at.

B: Umm. That's nice. How much is it?

A: The price is here on the label. This one costs £4.99, I think. Yes, that's right. Would you like to try it on?

B: Yes, I think I will.

A: Would you like to come this way? [Pause] Does it fit?

A: Yes, it's fine. I'll take it. Have you got any jeans that. . .

Unit 10   Saying thank you

i)   A: Right. Try that now.

    B: It still won't start.

    A: Yes, just a minute. Try it again.

    B: Fantastic.

    A: Right. You can switch it off now. You shouldn't have any more trouble.

    B: I don't know how to thank you. I really am very grateful to you for stopping to help me. I would have *been here all night* otherwise.

    A: Oh, that's all right. Don't mention it. Anyway I must be off. Goodbye. Have a safe journey.

    B: I will. And thanks again. Goodbye.

ii) A: Come on, Stephen. We must be going.

    B: Oh no, you don't have to go already, do you?

    C: I'm afraid we must, actually. We promised the babysitter we'd be back by midnight, and it'll take us half an hour to get home.

    D: I'll go and get your coats.

    B: Well, I'm glad you could come anyway.

    A: Well, thanks *very much indeed for inviting* us. We've had a marvellous time and I only wish we could stay longer. You must come round to our place some time. I'll give you a ring next week.

    B: Yes, all right. Thanks. Here's Martin with your coats. . .

iii) A: Right. Where shall we go now? We've seen the church and the modern art exhibition. I don't know what else there is here.

    B: How about some shops? I could do with some things to take back for the children.

    A: Umm, yes. O.K. Let's go down here and we'll come into the main street.

    B: You know, it really is good of you to *spend so much time* showing me around.

    A: Oh, that's all right. I'm enjoying it, actually. You know how it is. When you live in a town, you never really look at it yourself. Come on, let's go down here. . .

iv) A: Now, is there anything else I can tell you?

    B: No, I don't think so. And anyway, I've taken up quite enough of your time as it is.

    A: Oh, don't worry about that.

B: No, I really do appreciate what you've done, Professor Jameson. Thank you very much indeed for your *help*. You've certainly given me plenty of things to think about.

A: Well, all right. But if there's anything else I can do for you, do let me know.

B: I certainly will. Well thank you again, and I'll be in touch when I've looked through these books you've lent me.

A: All right. Goodbye for now then.

B: Goodbye, Professor Jameson.

Unit 11   Interview

Section 1

EW: Could you tell a bit about, er, why you wanted to be a doctor and how you first got into the medical profession?

DG: Well you've asked a rather strange person a pretty standard question. I happened to be doing languages for my 'A' levels at school and I decided that I didn't think there was a great deal of future in the study of languages so I decided that I'd change over to some scientific subject that I felt might be useful, and after a great deal of difficulty got accepted at medical school. Found it very difficult to get going but eventually succeeded and was perfectly happy. I certainly found the ability at least to appreciate other forms of things than purely basic science has been very helpful in the practice of medicine.

EW: So you mean you actually went into medical school or university without any 'A' levels in scientific subjects.

DG: At all, that's right. The first morning the lecturer wrote up some chemical formula on the board, which was the first chemistry lecture I'd ever been to. As far as I was concerned, she might have been putting it up in Egyptian hieroglyphics – it didn't mean a thing. That was a long time ago!

EW: So you had a lot of sort of personal, individual work to do, to catch up with everyone else then.

DG: Yes, it was very hard but the university I was at, which was Sheffield, had a kind of special class for what you might have called lame ducks such as myself and there was a retired watchmaker, there was a chemist, there was a dentist, there were a couple of nurses – people who'd come to do medicine in later life having taken up other things. So I think they looked after us well and most of us in the end managed to get through.

EW: And, er, you eventually qualified, er. . .

DG: Yes, when I qualified in Sheffield, way back in 1960, I was then actually so interested in the general aspects of medicine that I joined a special practice at the University of Manchester that was teaching general practice, and I was there for four years – thoroughly enjoyed it, it was teaching medical students and being involved very closely with the academic side of medical practice. And from then on I went on to student health service work back in my former university of Sheffield and then came down here to Reading twelve years ago.

Section 2

EW: Could you tell me something about the differences in being a medical doctor when you first started as opposed to what the work involves now?

DG: Yes, I think most of them are technological – strangely enough. You could probably say that medicine itself hasn't changed for the last four, five thousand years in terms of what the doctor actually does, apart from the tools with which he is endowed as a result of scientific developments. For example, when I qualified in 1960, the oral contraceptive pill was only just being used, so. . . and many of the antibiotics which currently we splash around like. . . like confetti amongst the patients had only just been developed – at least penicillin had been around for about ten or fifteen years. So there was that side, the enormous changes in the pharmacology of treatment. And secondly, many of the diagnostic tests, which nowadays one so simply orders from the hospital on a little white card, were ones which formerly could never be done because they were too complicated, or there was no way of performing the analysis. So medicine really has developed as a result of technology. The best example of that is sort of automated analysis of blood tests. Instead of having a technician now to look down a slide of a blood film, you put it in a machine which reads the slide automatically and records the result and the number of cells. So everything is done mechanically and automatedly. The next stage into which medicine is going is the same sort of way with statistical analysis of the records and computerisation of records and analysis of what medical care is being delivered to the patient. But in a way the doctor is the intermediary between the science and the patient. And that's really the role that hasn't changed.

EW: Would you say that these developments are making the doctor's job easier or more difficult – or simply different?

DG: I think simply different. They may, however, be making the doctor more remote from the patient, and I think many patients can appreciate this. Often they will hark back to their old family doctor who used to visit and sit for half an hour with the child sitting on their knee playing with the doctor's gold watch and they were the family friend and so on. What one has to remember was that in those days the doctor really hadn't got anything else to offer but his company, his presence and his comforting, . . . a sort of solicitation to make the patient feel happy whilst, hopefully, they survived their illness. Because he didn't have any magic medicines or pills to do it. Nowadays the patient will complain of the fact that: 'Oh well I was cured by the doctor whose name I didn't quite catch, who was there for $2\frac{1}{2}$ minutes and gave me a prescription. And 24 hours later as a result of the pink pills I was given I was better,' Er. . . so the doctor has become more remote because the science of therapeutics has become much more efficient.

EW: By therapeutics there, what. . .?

DG: I really mean therapeutics in the sense of the ability to treat an illness with a specific form of medicine which is designed to deal with it. The best example would be, take something like pneumonia. When I was a medical student, patients with pneumonia were being admitted to hospital – pneumonia being the serious disease of inflammation of the lungs. And they were ill for four or five days and they were in hospital for a fortnight then they were discharged and they were convalescent for another fortnight. Now, you could say that hardly any cases of pneumonia are ever in hospital because most patients, when they get a bad cold, are given antibiotics by their doctor so they never develop pneumonia.

Section 3

EW: Could you tell me whether you foresee, in the future, an explosion in private practice, and if so, what's the effect there's going to be on the National Health.

DG: That's a very difficult question to answer, because you could say that there are certain levels in the community, usually the higher social economic income groups who are very unhappy with the National Health Service, because they want more time from their doctor, they want to have their operation in a week that suits them, not when they're sent for by the hospital. They want to have a private bed in the hospital, with their own television and visiting hours at any time. And then, in a sense, they want to pay for this. Now the opportunities to buy this have in the past been limited by the facilities available under the National Health Service. And now that the National Health Service, because of political change, is virtually cancelling all the opportunities for private care inside the hospitals of the National Health Service, private hospitals are being built up and down the country. So in a way it is growing by its side. I wouldn't forecast an explosion. The simple reason is that it is so expensive. The average cost today, for example, of a private bed in one of the private hospitals is about £150 a day. Now there are not many people who can afford that kind of fee. Not many people can afford it. A lot of people are joining private insurance schemes to do this.

EW: Yes, I was going to mention that.

DG: Mm. . . but the private insurance schemes, you see, are costing people between £70 and £80 a year – perhaps more, depending on how much they choose to insure themselves for. So I think one can say that the National Health Service will continue as it has, with a variety of perhaps somewhat, er, regrettable deteriorations as a result of political change and I think private medical care will continue in the same way but separate from the NHS.

Unit 12 Travelling

A: [picks up receiver and dials].
B: Hello, Mick's taxis.
A: Oh, hello. I'd like to book a taxi please, to take me to the station tomorrow morning.
B: What time do you want to go?
A: I have to be at the station by 7.30.
B: I'm sorry. We're completely booked up then. We've nothing available until 9 o'clock. Sorry.

A: Oh well, I'd better leave it then. Thank you.
B: Thank You. Goodbye.
A: What a nuisance. I'll have to try another firm. Here we are. ABC Taxis.
C: Hello, ABC Taxis. Can I help you?
A: Hello, I'd like to book a taxi to the station tomorrow morning, please. I have to be there by 7.30.
C: 7.30? I see. Where is it from?
A: From Weston. 32 Hall Lane, Weston.
C: So we'll have to pick you up about 7 o'clock, then.
A: Yes, that would be fine.
C: Yes, I think we can manage that. What name is it please?
A: Hunt, Mrs Hunt.
C: O.K. Mrs Hunt. We'll see you tomorrow morning at 7 o'clock, then, Oh, just a minute. What was the address again? Was it 33 Hall Lane you said?
A: No, 32.
C: 32. Right. Goodbye. Thank you.
A: Goodbye.

Unit 12   Inviting and suggesting

i)   A: By the way, Sally, how are you going to get home from the party tomorrow?
     B: I don't know really. It's quite a problem. The last train to London leaves at 9.30, and that's far too early to leave.
     A: I'll tell you what. Why not *come and sleep at our house*?
     B: That's very kind of you. But I don't want to be a nuisance.
     A: It's no trouble. We've got a spare bed, you're very welcome.
     B: Well, if you're sure. . . then I'd like to. . .

ii) A: Hello, Gary? Oh, hello. It's Colin here.
     B: Ah, Colin. I thought I recognised your voice.
     A: Listen, Gary. Would you like *to come round to dinner on Friday*? We're having some friends round and we'd be very pleased if you could join us.
     B: Well, that sounds great. Yes, I'd love to. What kind of time?
     A: Oh, about eight. If that's O.K?
     B: That's fine. And thanks again.

iii) A: Hello, I'm sorry I'm late. There were some letters I had to finish at the office.
     B: That's O.K. I've only just arrived myself. Now, what are we going to do? Do you feel like a bit of fresh air? How about *going for a walk by the river*?
     A: Yes, I wouldn't mind that. Being at the office all day long has given me a headache. We could stop at the pub on the way back.
     B: Good idea. Let's go then. . .

iv) A: Well, what are we going to do then?
   B: I don't know. There's nothing on the telly, the theatre's all booked up, and I don't feel like just going to the pub.
   A: What's on at the cinema?
   B: Now there's an idea. Let's go and *see that horror film on at the Odeon.*
   A: Yes, that *is* a good idea – a good horror film.
   B: O.K. It starts at 8.00, I think, and it takes about half an hour to get to the Odeon, so we'd better hurry, Come on. . .

Unit 13   Trains and tubes

A: Can I help you?
B: Yes. How do I get to Chancery Lane, please?
A: Oh, that's simple. Take the Central Line eastbound. It's only three stops.
B: Thank you.
C: Could you tell me how to get to Lancaster Gate, please.
A: Lancaster Gate. Yes. Take the Central Line westbound. It's the stop after Marble Arch.
C: I see. The stop after Marble Arch. Right. Thank you.
D: Excuse me, how do I get to High Street, Kensington, please.
A: Umm. It's a bit complicated actually. Look, take the Central Line westbound as far as Notting Hill Gate. Then change on to the District or Circle line southbound. It's one stop after Notting Hill Gate.
D: Just let me check that. Central Line to Notting Hill Gate, then District or Circle Line southbound.
A: That's right.
D: Fine. Thanks very much.

Unit 13   Saying yes and no to invitations

i)   A: You know, sometimes I could kill my husband. He's so untidy.
    B: Yes, I know. Mine's the same. Do you know, in all the years we've been married he's never once done the washing up.
    A: It's terrible, isn't it.
    B: Oh, by the way, that reminds me. It's our anniversary on Friday. How about you and George coming round for drinks?
    A: Thanks a lot. That would *be nice.* Is anyone else coming?
    B: No, just you and George.
    A: O.K. So there won't be very much washing up to do. . .

ii) A: Trevor! Come in. Nice to see you.
    B: Actually, I can't stay. I just came to ask whether you and Pauline would like to come to London with us on Tuesday. We're going to do some shopping there, and I remember last week you said you wanted to go to London yourself.
    A: Oh, I'd love to come but I'm sorry, I'm *not free then.* In fact I begin work again on Monday.

    B: So soon? I thought you were on holiday till the 27th.

    A: No such luck! No, next Monday at 9.00 I'll be back at work. . .

iii) A: How's the new job, Bill?

    B: Oh, it's fine, thanks. The only problem is, we haven't found a new house yet. So I have a long journey to work every morning.

    A: That must be quite a nuisance. Listen, I know a very good estate agent in Winton. In fact he's a friend of mine. I'm going round to see him on Friday evening. Why don't you come along?

    B: Yes, I'd *love to*. What sort of time?

    A: Well, I said I'd be there about 8.00, so I'll pick you up at 7.30.

    B: Fine. Good. I'll be waiting. . .

iv) A: Hello, Derek. It's Don here. Look, the reason I'm ringing is to ask whether you're free on Wednesday. I bought two tickets for the theatre and unfortunately Anne can't come now. I thought you might like to come.

    B: Oh, I'm afraid *I can't*. I'd love to of course, but I'm babysitting actually.

    A: Babysitting! I thought only women did that!

    B: Not in this household. Judy's going to her evening class, so I've got to stay at home and look after Tony.

    A: Well, rather you than me, that's all I can say. . .

Unit 14 Cars

i) A: Good afternoon, sir. Can I help you?

    B: Umm. I'd like to hire a car for a few days.

    A: Yes, of course. What sort did you want?

    B: Well, it depends what you've got. What sort have you got available?

    A: Well, we've got Minis, Allegros – or if you want something bigger, we've got Princesses.

    B: No, no, I don't need anything big. It's only for me.

ii) B: How much is a Mini?

    A: Well there's a £50 deposit. And then it's £10 per day + 3p per mile.

    B: Umm. Does that include insurance?

    A: No, I'm afraid comprehensive insurance is £2 per day extra.

    B: And I still have to buy petrol.

    A: Oh yes, I'm afraid so.

iii) B: Isn't it possible to pay a flat rate? I'd rather not pay a mileage charge. 3p per mile is pretty expensive if you go a long way.

    A: Yes, if you want to you can pay £15 per day. Then you have unlimited mileage.

    B: Umm. That's probably better. I plan to do about 150 miles a day. So I'll save money with the flat rate, won't I? Yes, O.K., well I'll take a Mini on the flat rate then.

    A: Right, well if you can just let me have a few details – and the deposit – I'll get you the keys.

Unit 14 Making arrangements

i) A: Are you ready then, Ted?
   B: Sorry, I'm afraid I'm going to be at least another hour.
   A: Oh, well, we'd better meet in town in that case.
   B: O.K. What sort of time?
   A: Shall we *make it 5.00* in front of the library?
   B: 5.00 in front of the library. Yes that's fine.
   A: Good. That'll give me a chance to take my library books back before we meet. See you later. . .

ii) A: Are you coming to the concert tonight, Janet?
    B: Yes, I am actually. I'm going with Paul.
    A: Why don't we go over together then. I'm going with George.
    B: Fine. Whereabouts shall we meet?
    A: Let me see. Let's *say by the traffic lights* in Queen's Road at about 7.00.
    B: O.K. By the traffic lights at about 7.00. Now I must fly. I promised to meet Paul for coffee at 10.00, and it's ten past already.

iii) A: Hello Dick. Roger here.
     B: Oh hello, Roger. I was just going to phone you actually. About the meeting next week.
     A: Well, that's just why I'm phoning. I only heard about it a few minutes ago. You're going, I suppose?
     B: Yes, of course. How are we going to get there?
     A: Let's go by bus, shall we?
     B: No, I'll *pick you up* at about 7.00.
     A: O.K. That's very kind of you. My house at 7.00 then. I'm certainly looking forward to the meeting.
     B: Yes, it should be interesting. Well, see you next week, then. Thanks for phoning.
     A: O.K. 'Bye. . .

iv) A: Hello, Mr Brown?
    B: Speaking.
    A: Oh, hello. It's Mrs Knowlson here. Professor Wilkinson's secretary. Professor Wilkinson has an appointment with you this afternoon, I believe.
    B: Yes, that's right. At 4.30.
    A: Well, the reason I'm phoning is to ask whether that could be made 4.45 instead. Professor Wilkinson has a committee meeting which may not finish until later than he expected.
    B: Yes, that's fine. I've no other appointments this afternoon, so it's all the same to me.
    A: Good. So *shall we say 4.45* then?
    B: Yes, all right.
    A: Thank you. Goodbye.

Unit 15 Interview

Section 1

KM: What exactly do you do? I mean, what does your job consist of?

DR: At this moment in time, as I say, it's looking after the Railway's image, generally, er, dealing with public complaints – this is one of the things, one of my important aspects and sides of it. Not dealing with the publicity side, and then, er, dealing with, erm, any promotional type things, special features that come along. I issue press releases, do this sort of thing, get what I can in the media, blackmail some of my newspaper friends in the Reading area by buying them copious pints of beer and saying, 'There's a good story here', or 'There isn't a good story there.'

KM: Dealing with complaints, you said. That's an interesting thing. What sort of complaints do you get?

DR: Oh, all sorts of complaints, from all sorts of people, from all walks of life. People who complain about the rudeness of staff. Some people write in rhyme and write all sorts of things, er, about their train service. Other people are a little bit more, er, rude and say that we don't know what we're doing. We don't know what we're talking about. A lot of people write and say, well, they missed the last train because of the rudeness or the unhelpfulness of staff, and they want their taxi-fare back and this sort of thing. So the whole thing centres around keeping the temperature down as far as I'm concerned, probably judging whether some people are pulling a fast one for some taxi fare or not. Er, if I, er, if it's debatable, well it's like the old radio show, 'Give them the money, Barney' and it keeps everybody quiet. And this is how we go.

KM: So you have to investigate the complaints, I mean, and where possible you do try to smooth things out.

DR: Yes. If there's a . . . the staff are rude, they're often disciplined, and, er, you know a black mark goes on their record sheet. This type of thing.

KM: Umm. You, er, this is an interesting thing about the railways, isn't it, that, er, the staff in a sense are very exposed to the public all the time.

DR: Well, er, this is a question of the inner workings as Dr Beeching mentioned. Everybody sees the railway activity as it's being done. You see porters at work, you see ticket collectors at work, you see drivers, you see guards, you see everybody doing their own particular job. You even see shunters. The only people you don't see, of course, are the maintenance people who look after the trains and batteries and electric lights and this sort of thing.

KM: And people like yourself.

DR: Yes, and the backroom people, there's bound to be that. But there are more people in the frontline on British Rail than there are in other industries, er, such as baked beans for instance. You don't see the beans produced, you don't see them manufactured, all you see is the tin of beans on the, er, supermarket shelf. Er, so you can help yourself. If you like one variety better than another, you go and choose that. But you can't do that with the railways. You're reliant on what we produce, you're reliant on what our staff produce.

Section 2

KM: There is an element there about competition though, isn't there? Because British Railways are a nationalised industry, there's only one railway system in the country. If you don't like a particular can of baked beans, you can go and buy another, but if you don't like a particular railway, well you can't go and use another.

DR: Some of my, er, people who write to me say this. They say that if you didn't have a monopoly, you wouldn't be able to do the things you do. Well I don't think we do anything deliberately to upset our customers. In fact I'm sure we don't. We have particular problems. Since 1946 when the Transport Act came in, we were nationalised, we then became Government owned.

KM: Do you think that is a good thing? Has it been a good thing for the railways, do you think, to be nationalised?

DR: Oh, I think so, yes. Because in general, modes of transport all round, let's face the fact. The car arrived, the car is here to stay. There's no question about that.

KM: So, I mean. . ., so what you're saying then is that if the railways hadn't been nationalised, they would simply have disappeared.

DR: Oh I think they would have done. They are disappearing fast in America, parts of America from what I read through international journals. Er, the French railways lose £1,000 million a year, the German railways £2,000 million a year. But you see, those Governments are prepared to pour money into the transport system to keep it going.

KM: So in a sense you're caught between two extremes, on the one hand trying to, well, not exactly perhaps to make money, but at least not to lose too much money, and on the other hand you've got to provide the best service that you possibly can.

DR: This is true. We know for a fact that the, in this particular area, the Twyford–Henley branch loses money. It doesn't pay in any shape or form. The, er, Slough–Windsor branch loses money. The Ealing–Greenford branch loses money. . .

KM: But all these presumably have a social value.

DR: Yes, they have a social, and this is where it comes in, a social benefit and there is a social grant from the Government to the railways to keep these lines open. And this sort of thing.

KM: Right.

Section 3

KM: Despite the cutbacks though, you're saying you're working on last year's money, erm, there is quite a lot of new equipment coming on to the railways, things like these new High Speed Trains, that are working. Are these having, er, a great effect?

DR: Oh yes, we're delighted with the High Speed Trains, er, although some of our commuters aren't because it's meant that we've had to alter some of the services to fit these in. But it doesn't alter the fact that since they were introduced, two years ago, our receipts on inter-city travel have gone up 15%.

KM: 15%?

DR: 15%, which is pretty good; and er. . .

KM: Why, why do you think this is particularly? Is it just the speed or. . .?

DR: I think so, yes. Most people want faster journey times between the time they leave home and the time they get back. Most people do not want to drive, I find, with business people. If you travel by train, at least you can have a drink, at least you can do some work. Er, people moan sometimes about railway coffee, and all the rest of it. We have in fact brought the price down just to prove our good will.

KM: These High Speed Trains are, what, mainly orientated towards the businessman, then from what you're saying?

DR: Yes, yes.

KM: Is there anything that British Rail can do to make this sort of service available to, well, to private people, people who can't afford the fares charged. . .?

DR: Well we do, basically. We don't charge any extra to go on the High Speed Train. We charge normal, conventional fares.

KM: This is quite interesting actually, because that's rather different from the situation in a lot of other countries, the fact that you don't charge extra to go on specified trains. Is it then, it is then the case isn't it that, erm, to travel from A to B by train in Britain costs the same. . .

DR: That is what we are aiming at. We're not aiming to con everybody out of all their money. What we're aiming at is to provide a service. This is the thing, and we feel that, rather than reduce fares, as people want us to do, and as you know, if you reduce fares to a certain extent, you've got to get X number of extra passengers to make up the leeway before you even make a profit. And there's no guarantee you'll ever do this. So the thing is to provide facilities now, our existing facilities, to such an extent that people will not be able to resist them anyway and they will travel.

KM: Do you think this business of fares and prices. I mean you've argued, O.K., that it doesn't make sense overall to reduce fares. But, as I said a moment ago, in a lot of European countries there are supplements which are paid for travel on express trains, which means that perhaps on ordinary trains the fares can be significantly lower. Do you think that that is a possible system that might be worth thinking about in this country, or are there definite reasons why it wouldn't work?

DR: Well, I think it goes back to the reduced fare arrangement. I think there are definite reasons why it wouldn't work. It wouldn't work because we wouldn't get, we would have the same number of people paying less for their journey. I don't think we would get the additional fare. What we want to do is attract people to our existing services. Altogether, supplements and all the rest of it cost an awful lot for admin. and chitties and various forms people have to make out, and I don't think that these things are on at all. Our seat reservation system. . . We did have a supplement system on the 'Golden Hind' which ran from Paddington. It was a non-stop train to Exeter in the evening. The only reason we did that was because it was such a limited-load train, that you had to try and put a 50p supplement on to keep people off quite frankly, not to make money to get people on. It was as simple as that.

KM: Umm.